St. Augustine
and St. Johns County
A Historical Guide

William R. Adams

Pineapple Press, Inc.
Sarasota, Florida

Ponce de Leon Hotel (Flagler College)

Pineapple Press, Inc.
P.O. Box 3889
Sarasota, Florida 34230
www.pineapplepress.com

Library of Congress Cataloging-in-Publication Data

Adams, William R., Dr.
 St. Augustine and St. Johns County : a historical guide / William R. Adams. -- 1st ed.
     p. cm.
 ISBN 978-1-56164-432-2 (pbk. : alk. paper)
1. Saint Augustine (Fla.)--Guidebooks. 2. Saint Johns County (Fla.)--Guidebooks. 3. Historic sites--Florida--Saint Augustine--Guidebooks. 4. Historic sites--Florida--Saint Johns County--Guidebooks. I. Title. II. Title: Saint Augustine and Saint Johns County.
 F319.S2A28 2009
 917.59'180464--dc22
                                        2008033411

First Edition
10 9 8 7 6 5 4 3 2 1

Design by Shé Hicks
Printed in the United States of America

Contents

Acknowledgments 7
Introduction 9
Historic Periods 11

Area One—North Colonial City 12

Castillo de San Marcos National Monument 14
Visitor Information Center 15
Colonial City Historic District 16
Restoration Area 17
Cubo Line of Defense 18
City Gate 19
Public Burying Ground (Huguenot Cemetery) 20
Genopoly House ("Oldest Schoolhouse") 21
Avero House (St. Photios Shrine) 22
de Mesa Sánchez House 23
Rodríguez-Avero-Sánchez House 24
Paredes-Dodge House 25
Peña-Peck House 26
Government House 27
Colonial Town Plaza (*Plaza de la Constitución*) 28
Constitution Monument (*Monumento de la Constitución*) 29
Cathedral Basilica of St. Augustine 30
Exchange Bank Building 31
Trinity Episcopal Church 32
Bridge of Lions 33

Area Two—South of the Plaza 34

Seguí–Kirby Smith House 36
Ximenez-Fatio House 37
González-Alvarez House ("Oldest House") 38
Tovar House 39
St. Francis Barracks 40
National Cemetery 41
Fernández-Llambias House 42
O'Reilly House 43
Col. Upham Cottage 44
Bronson Cottage 45
Prince Murat House 46

Canova House   47
Palm Row   48
Lincolnville Historic District   49
St. Cyprian's Episcopal Church   50
St. Benedict the Moor Church   51

Area Three—West of the Colonial City   52

Alcazar Hotel   54
Lightner Musuem   55
Casa Monica Hotel   56
Ponce de Leon Hotel (Flagler College)   57
Villa Zorayda (Zorayda Castle)   58
Xavier Lopez House   59
Markland   60
Solla-Carcaba Cigar Factory   61
Flagler Memorial Presbyterian Church   62
Ingraham House (Presbyterian Manse)   63
Model Land Company Historic District   64
Ancient City Baptist Church   65
Grace United Methodist Church   66
Tolomato Cemetery   67

Area Four—Abbott Tract and North City   68

Abbott Tract Historic District   70
Warden Castle (Ripley's "Believe It or Not!" Museum)   71
Mission of Nombre de Dios   72
Fountain of Youth Park   73
The Old Jail   74

Area Five—Anastasia Island   76

Oglethorpe Battery Park   78
St. Augustine Alligator Farm   79
St. Augustine Lighthouse and Keeper's Quarters   80
Old Spanish Well and Chimney   81
Old Spanish Quarries   82
Anastasia State Recreation Area   83
Fish Island Site   84
Summer Haven   85
Butler Beach and Frank Butler Park   86
Fort Matanzas National Monument   87
Massacre of the French, Matanzas Inlet   88

Area Six—St. Johns County   90
O'Brien-Kelley House   92
Treaty Park   93
St. Ambrose Catholic Church   94
Hastings   95
Faver Dykes State Park   96
Fort Mosé   97
Guana River State Park   98
William Bartram Trail   99
Picolata   100

Unmarked Historic Sites in St. Johns County   102
Osceola Capture Site   104
Moultrie   104
Old Kings Road   105
Dixie Highway   105
Theatrical Troupe Massacre Site   106
Operation Pastorius   106
Switzerland   107
Fort San Diego, or Diego Plains   107

Index   108

Fort Matanzas National Monument

Government House

Acknowledgments

Paul Weaver, a historic preservation consultant who co-authored the first version of this book, provided continuing help with this volume. Dr. Cécile-Marie Sastre, a historical authority on colonial military architecture, contributed invaluable information on the many sites that fall into that category.

Historical information compiled by the research staff of the Historic St. Augustine Preservation Board in comprehensive city and county architectural surveys which that now-defunct state organization conducted from 1978 to 1985 constituted the richest body of research for this book.

Thanks are due Mike Strock for correcting the historical description of the Trinity Episcopal Church, Dr. Will Spencer for information about St. Cyprian's Episcopal Church, and Eric Johnson for reviewing the textual sketch of the Nombre de Dios Mission grounds. Gratitude is owed, finally, to the many authors of articles and books, thick and thin, about the history of St. Augustine and its environs that provided background material for site descriptions. Information pertaining to some historical attractions, such as hours and days of operation, came from brochures and pamphlets.

The color photographs for this revised version of the book were, for the most part, shot in 2008 by Angelika Lochner. Others were taken from the files of the St. Augustine and St. Johns County Visitor Convention Bureau with its permission.

Alcazar Hotel (City Hall)

City Gate

Introduction

St. Augustine's reputation as America's oldest city and its Old World Spanish character have attracted visitors for nearly two centuries. From its settlement in 1565 through the twenty-first century, this small locale has at times played an outsized role in the political, social, and economic life of Florida and the United States. Its historic resources reflect the area's historical significance. They attract sightseers looking to visit places and buildings that reflect the area's more than four centuries of recorded history.

The significance of many places and buildings that testify to St. Augustine's and St. Johns County's historic past, such as the Castillo de San Marcos and Ponce de Leon Hotel (now part of Flagler College), are obvious. Others remain relatively unknown, often revealed only by the presence of a historic marker.

Visiting a place where history was made puts the visitor in touch with the past. Standing on the actual ground where something of importance happened helps to recreate a feeling of historic time and circumstance, so long as there remains some part of the physical surroundings that testifies to the historical event.

The buildings and places described in this book do not, in their telling, portray the full history of this region. Some were selected for their architecture, others for their historical importance, and a few as reminders of an event or historic setting that is disappearing amid the voracious modern development overtaking St. Johns County. Some are located in remote places, virtually inaccessible.

A few in the latter category may no longer be worth the visit. Earlier versions of this book, published in 1992 and 2005, describe sites that have since all but disappeared. Because they form a fascinating part of the area's history, however, some are retained in this edition without illustration (there is really nothing to picture) or precise location directions. Their inclusion represents a small attempt to preserve historic memory.

Among them are the Osceola Capture site, once marked only by a post sunk into the ground; the Theatrical Troupe Massacre site, designated by a bronze sign stuck along a roadway miles into the countryside; and Diego Plains, where no vestige of the historic setting remains. Those sites and others described as "Unmarked Historic Sites in St. Johns County" have essentially lost their historic "sense of place" and, in most cases, no longer even warrant a historic marker.

Many sites described in this book are found on privately owned property. Unless they are publicly accessible or the visitor has express permission to enter the property, such sites should be viewed only from the public right-of-way. We urge visitors to respect the privacy of ownership where access is not clearly permitted.

Spanish accents have been retained where they are historically justified. If the Spanish name or word has been anglicized (such as the name of nineteenth-century soldier and politician Joseph Hernandez), the accent is not applied. Where a date cannot be precisely set, the abbreviation of the Latin preposition circa (ca.), meaning "about," is used.

Readers should understand the distinction between the often-used terms "restored" and "reconstructed." A restored building is a standing structure that has been accurately rehabilitated to resemble its appearance at some point in its historic past. A reconstructed building is one that has been built from the ground up to look like a building that once stood on the same ground at a previous time.

For this publication, we have divided St. Johns County into discrete areas and organized the historic places within each in a geographically sequential fashion that will facilitate travel from one to another.

Cathedral of St. Augustine

Historic Periods

In the descriptions of places and buildings that follow, the reader will encounter references to specific periods of Florida history. They are:

First Spanish Period (1565–1763)
The city's longest historic period yet, this era of Florida's history began with the settlement of St. Augustine and ended when Spain was forced to relinquish the colony to Great Britain at the end of the French and Indian War (1756–1763). Twice during that long period, in 1702 and again in 1740, the British mounted serious attempts to take St. Augustine by force, failing each time. Throughout its first two centuries, St. Augustine was the only European settlement of note within the Spanish colony of Florida. Not until the year 2056 will the Stars and Stripes have flown over Florida as long as did the flag of Spain. Sixteeen buildings survive from the First Spanish Period.

British Period (1763–1784)
Great Britain's hold over Florida lasted a mere two decades, a time encompassing the American Revolutionary War. The Treaty of Paris at the war's end returned Florida to Spain, which had supported the victorious American rebels. The British divided Florida into two colonies—East Florida, with its capital at St. Augustine, and West Florida, which British authorities administered from Pensacola.

Second Spanish Period (1784–1821)
The Spanish returned to Florida twenty-one years after they had departed, regaining the colony as reward for their victorious alliance with the rebellious Americans in the thirteen northern colonies. The years that followed were troubled ones for Spain, which was occupied at home by the invading armies of Napoleon Bonaparte and shaken by the loosening of colonial bonds in the Western Hemisphere. The Adams-Onís Treaty, signed in 1819, transferred ownership of Florida from Spain to the United States, although the American occupation did not actually begin until 1821.

Colonial Period (1565-1821)
This encompasses all the periods before the Amerian Period. Thirty-six builidngs survive from the Colonial Period.

American Period (1821–Present)
Florida remained a territory of the United States from 1821 until 1845, when it achieved statehood. During that time, the U.S. government fought a long and costly war against the Seminole Indians, known as the Second Seminole War (1835–1842). Throughout most of the Civil War (1861–1865), Federal troops occupied St. Augustine. In the late years of the nineteenth century, St. Augustine embarked upon a great architectural renaissance. That period of the city's history, named the Flagler Era for the entrepreneur who inspired it, lasted from 1886 to about 1913, when Henry Flagler died.

Area One
North Colonial City

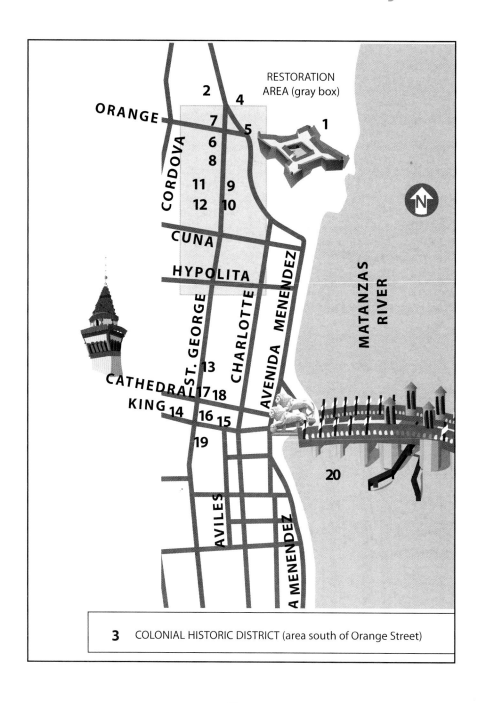

RESTORATION
AREA (gray box)

ORANGE

2

4

7

5

1

CORDOVA

6

8

11

9

12

10

CUNA

HYPOLITA

ST. GEORGE

CHARLOTTE

AVENIDA MENENDEZ

MATANZAS RIVER

CATHEDRAL

13

17 18

KING

14

16

15

19

20

AVILES

A MENENDEZ

3 COLONIAL HISTORIC DISTRICT (area south of Orange Street)

1 Castillo de San Marcos National Monument 14
2 Visitor Information Center 15
3 Colonial City Historic District 16
4 Restoration Area 17
5 Cubo Line of Defense 18
6 City Gate 19
7 Public Burying Ground (Huguenot Cemetery) 20
8 Genopoly House ("Oldest Schoolhouse") 21
9 Avero House (St. Photios Shrine) 22
10 de Mesa Sánchez House 23
11 Rodríguez-Avero-Sánchez House 24
12 Paredes-Dodge House 25
13 Peña-Peck House 26
14 Government House 27
15 Colonial Town Plaza
   (*Plaza de la Constitución*) 28
16 Constitution Monument
   (*Monumento de la Constitución*) 29
17 Cathedral Basilica of St. Augustine 30
18 Exchange Bank Building 31
19 Trinity Episcopal Church 32
20 Bridge of Lions 33

Castillo de San Marcos 1672–1695

Location
On the waterfront, along U.S. A1A near its intersection with Orange Street

Visitor information
Maintained by the U.S. National Park Service and open daily to visitors. Plan your visit before 4:00 p.m. Parking at the site is limited. Ample parking is available at the City's Visitor Information Center parking facility, less than a block away. Guardrooms surrounding the interior courtyard of the Castillo contain exhibits and a gift store.

History
Construction of the Castillo de San Marcos began in 1672, little more than a century after the founding of St. Augustine. A menacing English presence in the Carolinas after 1670 persuaded the Spanish Crown to erect the fortress and strengthen the city's defenses. The Castillo's

VC

physical integrity and structural splendor remain largely intact more than three centuries after the initial phase of construction ended in 1695. The fortress was fashioned from coquina, a conglomerate shell stone dug from quarries on Anastasia Island, some two miles distant and on the other side of the Matanzas River. On two occasions, in 1702 and 1740, attacking armies from the English colonies to the north failed to capture the Castillo. Upon transfer of Florida to the United States in 1821, the U.S. War Department, new owner of the fortress, renamed it Fort Marion in honor of Revolutionary War hero Francis Marion. It remained an active U.S. military post until 1900. In 1933, the U.S. Department of the Interior assumed stewardship of the Castillo, which it subsequently designated a national monument. The Castillo is the oldest masonry fortification in North America and the best-preserved example of Spanish colonial military architecture in the continental United States. The majestic Castillo historically reflects Spain's imperial presence in North America.

Visitor Information Center 1938

Location

12 Castillo Drive, at its intersection with San Marco Avenue, a long block east of the intersection of U.S. 1 and Castillo Drive

Visitor information

This building contains the city's principal information center for visitors, open seven days a week. Brochures explaining attractions and places of interest in the city may be found here. Information hosts are available to answer questions about restaurants, lodging, attractions, and directions. A four-story parking facility adjacent to the building provides ample parking for automobiles. It is the city's principal parking lot. The entrance to the lot is off Castillo Drive and Cordova Street. Two private transportation companies maintain ticket counters in the building.

History

The Visitor Information Center (VIC) is one of a few major buildings in the city constructed during the Depression Era of the 1930s. It was built under the auspices of the Works Progress Administration (WPA), a New Deal agency organized to alleviate unemployment. As such, it exemplifies the architectural contributions the WPA made to American communities during a difficult economic time. The building, designed by St. Augustine architect Fred A. Henderich, served as a community center until the 1950s, when the Chamber of Commerce began using it for visitor orientation. The building's location near the northern entrance to the colonial city and the Castillo de San Marcos positions it well for that purpose. Constructed of coquina, the most historically significant building material used in St. Augustine, the VIC has in the past quarter-century played an important role in tourism, which drives the city's economy. In 1991, the City of St. Augustine assumed responsibility for managing the building and its associated information services. A major renovation of the building's interior space and surrounding grounds was completed in 2006.

Colonial City Historic District ca.1572 to the present

Location

Orange Street forms the north boundary of the Colonial City Historic District. The west boundary runs southward eleven blocks along Cordova Street to San Salvador Street, its south boundary. Matanzas Bay forms the district's east boundary.

Visitor information

The rectangular, twenty-two-block Colonial City Historic District contains nearly all of the city's extant colonial-era historic resources, including the Castillo de San Marcos, the Restoration Area, the Plaza, and many other buildings and sites found in this guide. Visitors can obtain maps and literature describing places of interest in St. Augustine at the Visitor Information Center (see page 15), located at the north entry to this district. Spacious parking is available there, one block east of U.S. 1, along Castillo Drive.

History

The St. Augustine Colonial City Historic District (also called the Town Plan Historic District) contains within its boundaries the relatively small part of the modern city inhabited during the Colonial Period (1565–1821). The original landing of the Spanish colonizing expedition in 1565 took place a half-mile north of this district. In 1566 the settlement moved across the bay to Anastasia Island, where it remained until 1572 before returning to the mainland, close to what is now the Plaza. About 1596, following royal regulations, Spanish Governor Gonzalo Méndez de Canzo drafted an urban plan for the colonial town, making St. Augustine the oldest planned European community in North America. The outline of the colonial town, which in modern times contains some twenty-two urban blocks, remains essentially intact. Between 1704 and 1808, the Spanish constructed earthen defensive walls around the perimeter of this colonial *presidio,* or military garrison town, defining its boundaries. At its center is the Plaza, still the focus of urban life. This historic district embraces thirty-six extant buildings that date from the Colonial Period, as well as an impressive mix of architectural styles that portray every era of the city's more than four centuries of recorded history.

Restoration Area 1672 to the present

Location

The boundaries of the Restoration Area are not precisely defined, though St. George Street, from Orange Street to Hypolita Street, runs through its center. About six blocks in size, the Restoration Area is located immediately west of the Castillo de San Marcos, separated from the fortress by Florida Highway A1A.

Visitor information

St. George Street is a pedestrian-only street. Visitors to the Restoration Area, which includes numerous sites and buildings described in this volume, should park at the Visitor Information Center parking facility, a half-block north of the City Gate, which marks the entrance to the Restoration Area.

History

Settlement in this part of St. Augustine began with the construction of the Castillo de San Marcos in 1672. The Restoration Area, a six-block part of the north Colonial City, contains a number of original and reconstructed colonial-era buildings that thematically reflect the eighteenth and early nineteenth centuries. The modern program to restore the area to its colonial appearance commenced in 1935 under the auspices of the Carnegie Institute. In preparing for the celebration in 1965 of the city's four-hundredth anniversary, the state of Florida undertook to reconstruct elements of the colonial town. Under the auspices of the Historic St. Augustine Preservation Board, the state remained actively engaged in the Restoration Area until 1997, when it relinquished its role. Visitors will find within this area a "living history" museum known as the Colonial Spanish Quarter, which offers an interpretive introduction to life in colonial times. Many buildings along St. George Street contain gift shops, restaurants, bookstores, and other diversions for visitors. Maps, historical documents, and archaeological excavation of buried foundations provided a documentary basis for the accurate reconstruction in this part of the city of many colonial-era buildings that disappeared after 1821.

Cubo Line of Defense
ca. 1704–1835 (reconstructions made in 1965 and 2003)

Location

West lawn of the Castillo de San Marcos, at the intersection of Florida Highway A1A and Orange Street. The reconstructed section of the line runs from east to west upon the glacis, a sloping field of grass that surrounds the Castillo de San Marcos. At one time the Cubo Line continued on to the San Sebastian River, a distance of about half a mile.

Visitor information

The Cubo Line and the Santo Domingo Redoubt can be viewed at any time of day.

History

After English colonial troops under the command of Carolina Governor James Moore destroyed St. Augustine in 1702, the Spanish began erecting a series of defensive walls to protect the town. The first part of this system, the Cubo Line, constructed ca. 1704, essentially consisted of a vegetation-covered earthen parapet. Prickly plants such as palmettos and Spanish bayonet were planted on the line's outer face to repel attackers and discourage free-roaming livestock from climbing onto the parapet. The Cubo and Rosario Lines, which comprised the town wall, enclosed the colonial city on the north, west, and south. The section of the Cubo Line east of the Santo Domingo Redoubt formed the town's northern wall. From time to time, the Cubo Line was repaired or reconstructed, as were the rest of the City's defensive lines. Effectively, its military usefulness ended after the Second Seminole War (1835–1842), the last time the line was repaired.

A redoubt is a fortified position, either free-standing or placed along a line of entrenchment, capable of holding artillery. Reconstruction of the Santo Domingo Redoubt, located a few hundred feet west of the City Gate, was completed in 2003, a cooperative project of the City of St. Augustine, the Florida Department of State, and the National Park Service.

City Gate 1808

Location
The twin pillars known as the City Gate stand at the north end of St. George Street, where Florida Highway A1A intersects with Orange Street. The Castillo de San Marcos is located about three hundred yards to the east.

Visitor information
Visitors pass between the pillars on their walk from the Visitor Information Center, where parking is available, to the Restoration Area along St. George Street.

History
Upon construction of the Cubo Line in 1704, a wooden gate within the earthen parapet protected the town's northern entrance. This gateway marked the eastern terminal of the Camino Real, or Royal Highway, which proceeded westward to Apalache (in the vicinity of present-day Tallahassee) and beyond. The impressive coquina pillars, which once held the wooden gate that provided entrance to St. George Street, were erected in 1808. The Cubo Line itself required constant repair, but remained in use through the Second Seminole War (1835–1842). By the end of the Civil War (1865), the largely earthen walls had generally disintegrated, but the coquina pillars continued to stand. In 1906, a group of women prevented municipal officials from demolishing the pillars, offering an early example of concern for preserving the historic city. Two colorful parades each year, one in early spring and one in early December, featuring Spanish and English military re-enactment groups, recall the nightly colonial ceremony of locking the entry gate. The western part of the perimeter wall was called the Rosario Line. It ran about eleven blocks north to south along what is today Cordova Street. The City of St. Augustine has reconstructed a section of that earthen wall south of Orange Street.

Public Burying Ground (Huguenot Cemetery) 1821

Location
At the intersection of Orange Street and Avenida Menendez, north of the City Gate

Visitor information
The cemetery is closed to the public. It can be viewed from the south grounds of the Visitor Information Center and the sidewalks leading from there to the City Gate.

History
Under the Adams-Onís Treaty of 1819, Spain ceded Florida to the United States, which took formal possession of the former colony in 1821. Americans began migrating southward to St. Augustine, which under Spanish rule had been a Catholic town. That same year, when a yellow fever epidemic struck, the need for a public cemetery in which to bury members of Protestant faiths became quickly apparent. For that purpose, the City

Council selected a half-acre plot of ground north of the City Gate in a cleared area that federal surveyors had set aside as a town commons. The fever claimed 172 victims that year. The Presbyterian congregation acquired the cemetery in 1832. From then until 1887, when interments were discontinued, this cemetery served as St. Augustine's principal non-Catholic burying ground. Many significant historical names appear on its tombstones. The name "Huguenot," later attached to the cemetery, may have been popularized by author William Cullen Bryant, a visitor to St. Augustine, who in an 1872 booklet referred readers to the "old Huguenot Burying Ground." The cemetery, however, had no historical or other relationship to the French Huguenots who founded the short-lived settlement of Fort Caroline (north of Jacksonville on the south bank of the St. Johns River) in 1562. Tourism promoters probably stuck the name "Huguenot" to it.

Genopoly House ("Oldest Schoolhouse") ca. 1804

Location
14 St. George Street, at the north end of the Restoration Area, a half-block south of the City Gate

Visitor information
The privately owned building is accessible daily for an admission fee.

History
The oldest surviving wood-frame building in St. Augustine, constructed during the Second Spanish Period (1784–1821), the Genopoly House has for more than three quarters of a century stood on public

exhibit as the "Oldest Schoolhouse." Its builder, Juan Genopoly, a Greek carpenter and member of an ill-fated attempt to establish a British colony at New Smyrna populated by indentured servants from Italy, Greece, and Minorca, purchased the property in 1778 and undertook construction of the frame house about 1804. The building served a succession of inhabitants as a residence until the 1920s, when the growing commercialization of St. George Street prompted its owner to begin portraying the building as the "Oldest Wooden Schoolhouse." William J. Harris, a noted St. Augustine photographer, owned the building for a time before it was sold in the early 1930s to St. Augustine Mayor Walter B. Fraser, who was instrumental in organizing the city's restoration program in 1935.

All of the other colonial-era (1565–1821) buildings in St. Augustine feature stone-wall construction. Termites, humidity, heat, heavy rainfall, frequent lightning storms, and other forces of nature wreak havoc on historic buildings in Florida, especially wooden ones. For its age, the Genopoly House is a rare survivor.

Avero House (St. Photios Shrine) ca. 1735–1743

Location
41 St. George Street

Visitor information
The shrine is open daily to visitors. There is no admission fee.

History
The Avero House, constructed during the First Spanish Period (1565–1763), warrants recognition as the earliest surviving house of worship in North America associated with the Greek Orthodox faith. Upon abandoning the failed colony of New Smyrna in 1777, Greek immigrants who had arrived in Florida with the 1768 expedition fled to St. Augustine. They held their first religious service in the Ancient City within this building. As its contribution to the American Revolutionary War Bicentennial celebration, the Greek Orthodox Church of North America

restored the colonial-era building in the mid-1970s, creating the Shrine of St. Photios. The shrine commemorates the eighteenth-century Greek odyssey to North America and the congregation's beginnings in St. Augustine. In restoring the two-century-old building, craftsmen from Europe skillfully fashioned splendidly detailed mosaics and paintings that colorfully depict the history of Greeks in St. Augustine and America.

The residents of St. Augustine gave the name "Minorcan" indiscriminately to all of the immigrants who fled the failed New Smyrna colony in 1777, although only a minority of them were actually natives of the island of Minorca, near the Mediterranean coast of Spain. To this day, all of the descendants of those immigrants, including those of Italian and Greek national origin, proudly refer to themselves as Minorcans.

de Mesa-Sánchez House ca. 1740

Location
43 St. George Street, adjoining the St. Photios Shrine

Visitor information
The de Mesa-Sánchez House is one of nine reconstructed and restored historic buildings included within the Colonial Spanish Quarter Museum.

History
Antonio de Mesa, his wife, and seven children were the first inhabitants of this residence, which de Mesa—an employee of the Spanish Royal Treasury—built about 1740, sometime after his arrival in St. Augustine. The residence grew with each new owner, especially don Juan Sánchez, who owned it in the 1790s. Soon after the United States took control of Florida in 1821, James Lisk purchased the house and built an addition that integrated a detached kitchen into the main building. He also added a balcony overlooking St. George Street and painted the house a brilliant pink color, with ashlar scoring. It passed through the hands of many owners until 1935, when the house was converted to a tourist attraction called "the Old Spanish Inn."

To give it a look of antiquity, the owner stripped the stucco from its coquina walls. Within thirty years, intrusive moisture had all but ruined the interiors. The Historic St. Augustine Preservation Board purchased the house in 1976 and restored it to an early configuration that included a new exterior coat of pink stucco.

Coquina is a highly porous stone. Colonial-era Spanish builders quickly found that to protect the interiors of coquina-walled buildings against intrusive moisture, the exterior wall had to be covered with a water-resistant material. They used a locally made, lime-based stucco, applying it to both the exterior and interior walls. Modern owners of coquina-walled buildings continue to relearn the need for such protection.

Rodríguez-Avero-Sánchez House ca. 1753–1762

Location
52 St. George Street, across the street from the Colonial Spanish Quarter Museum

Visitor information
The Rodríguez-Avero-Sánchez House presently houses a gift store.

History
The construction date of this building, which was completed shortly before the British Period (1763–1784, the time of the American Revolution), establishes the Rodríguez-Avero-Sánchez House as one of the sixteen surviving buildings from the First Spanish Period (1565–1763). With walls fashioned of coquina stone, the building begins right at the street line, common to buildings of the Spanish colonial periods. It experienced some major changes shortly before the American Civil War (1861–1865), including the addition of a wood-frame second story. The building is one of a cluster of five colonial-era properties found in this part of the Restoration Area. The others include the adjoining Paredes-Dodge House, the Arrivas House (north of the Rodríguez-Avero-Sánchez House), and, across St. George Street to the east, the de Mesa-Sánchez House and the Avero House (St. Photios Shrine).

The colonial architecture of St. Augustine was influenced by a royal ordinance issued by the king of Spain in 1573 that directed the organization of new towns. The Spanish Crown's administrative rules decreed that in hot climates, town streets should be narrow, and added: "All town houses are to be so planned that they can serve as a defense or fortress against those who might attempt to create disturbances or occupy the town. Each house is to be so constructed that horses and household animals can be kept therein, the courtyards and stockyards being as large as possible to insure health and cleanliness."

Paredes-Dodge House 1808–1813

Location
54 St. George Street. The Paredes-Dodge House shares a common wall with the Rodríguez-Avero-Sánchez House to the north of it.

Visitor information
The Paredes-Dodge House, used as a retail gift store, is accessible daily.

History
Built between 1808 and 1813, this one-and-a-half-story Spanish Colonial building, located in the Restoration Area on St. George Street, is one of thirty-six surviving buildings dating from the Colonial Period (1565–1821). It was built by Juan Paredes, a mariner from Mallorca who purchased the lot in 1803, along with wall-sharing rights (*arrimo*) to the house north of his lot. Following the death of Paredes in 1813, his daughter sold the property to Pedro Fucha, who three weeks later also acquired the adjoining Rodríguez-Avero-Sánchez House. The two houses shared a common wall and, for a number of years in the nineteenth century, common ownership.

James P. Dodge, who purchased the building in 1900, billed it as "The Oldest House in America, 1565," despite its relatively youthful colonial age. His widow, Emma Dodge, sold the house to the St. Augustine Historical Society and Institute of Science (now the St. Augustine Historical Society) in 1934. For the past century and more, as St. Augustine's tourist industry expanded amid the

growth of automobile travel, the buildings along north St. George Street, like this one, were converted to commercial use. The Society sold the Paredes-Dodge House to the Historic St. Augustine Preservation Board in 1988.

Peña-Peck House ca. 1750

Location
143 St. George Street, at its intersection with Treasury Street

Visitor information
The St. George Street pedestrian mall ends one block south of this building. The Woman's Exchange Club maintains a small gift store in the Peña-Peck House and offers daily tours that enable visitors to view the period furnishings and artwork.

History
The stone walls of this building date to about 1750 and surround the house built for the Spanish Royal Treasurer, Juan Esteban de Peña, during the late years of the First Spanish Period (1565–1763). The acting governor of British East Florida from 1771 to 1774, Dr. John Moultrie Jr., lived here from 1772 to 1778. A South Carolina physician, Moultrie remained loyal to the British cause during the American Revolution, though his brother, William, served the rebel army as a general. In 1837, a Connecticut physician, Dr. Seth Peck, purchased the property and added a frame second story to the old walls. Peck died during a yellow fever epidemic in1841. For the next ninety-four years, his descendants continued living in the house. The last survivor of the family, Anna Gardner Burt, willed the property to the City of St. Augustine in 1931. Since that year, the Woman's Exchange Club, a volunteer organization founded in 1892 to which Anna Burt belonged, has maintained and exhibited the house. Recognized for more than a century as one of the city's finest houses, many of its extraordinary furnishings have, for the most part, been a part of its decor for over 150 years.

Government House ca. 1710

Location

10 Cathedral Place, between St. George Street and Cordova Street, on the west side of the Plaza. Government House is located at the south end of the St. George Street pedestrian mall, three blocks south of the Visitor Information Center.

Visitor information

The building's ground floor contains a museum displaying historical artifacts, many of them recovered from local archaeological digs.

History

Government House served as the home and headquarters for Spanish and British royal governors for two and a quarter centuries. In keeping with royal Spanish decree, its location on one side of the central plaza was prescribed in the plan for the town of St. Augustine, drafted about 1596 by the Spanish Governor of Florida, Gonzalo Méndez de Canzo. Invading Englishmen in 1702

destroyed the first house of the Royal Governor on the site. The Spanish at once rebuilt it. But when the Americans took control of the city in 1821, Government House again lay in ruins. Robert Mills (1781–1855), architect of the United States and the designer of the Washington Monument, drew the new plans for the building, retaining parts of the earlier walls. Government House acquired its present dimensions in 1935, when it was rebuilt by the Works Progress Administration for use as a post office and customs house. In 1964, the federal government transferred the building's title to the state of Florida. Since that year, it has served as the headquarters for the city's historic preservation administrators. During their epochal visit to St. Augustine on April 1, 2001, the king and queen of Spain made a public appearance on the building's east balcony, which overlooks the historic Plaza. King Juan Carlos spoke to a crowd of thousands gathered below him surrounding the historic monument to Spanish constitutional government (see page 29), which Juan Carlos restored in 1976 after a 162-year lapse.

Colonial Town Plaza (*Plaza de la Constitución*)
ca. 1596 to the present

Location
The Plaza stands at the center of the historic colonial town, one block west of the Bridge of Lions. Surrounding streets include Cathedral Place, King Street, and St. George Street.

Visitor information
The Plaza, a public square, is accessible day and night, seven days a week. Limited curbside parking is available along King Street and Cathedral Place.

History
The main plaza was a conspicuous part of every town or city in Spain and in the Spanish colonies of the Western Hemisphere. It provided the centerpiece for community life. The location of St. Augustine's plaza was set forth in the Town Plan, drafted about 1596 and promulgated by the Royal Governor a few years later. The grid pattern for the streets prescribed in the plan remains the prevailing pattern for modern streets in what had been the colonial city. Major government and religious buildings surrounded the Colonial Town Plaza during the colonial era. Within the rectangular block of land that contains the plaza now stand a public market, built about 1840, and several important monuments: the 1813 Constitution Monument,

a Confederate War Memorial, and a small memorial listing servicemen from St. Augustine who died in the wars of the twentieth century. Four artillery pieces, dating from the Mexican War and Civil War periods, are positioned in the Colonial Town Plaza. The gazebo in the plaza's center, erected in 1914, continues to provide a venue for public concerts. Archaeologists have excavated two colonial-era wells within the square, one in 1976 as a Bicentennial project and another in 1995, the latter dig conducted by the city archaeologist.

Constitution Monument
(Monumento de la Constitución) 1813

Location
The monument is located within the west end of the Plaza in downtown St. Augustine, surrounded by Cathedral Place, King Street, and St. George Street.

Visitor information
Limited curbside parking is available on adjacent streets (see Colonial Town Plaza).

History
The Constitution Monument was constructed in 1813, during the Second Spanish Period (1784–1821), to celebrate a newly formed constitutional government in Spain. On August 14, 1812, the Spanish Parliament issued a royal decree naming all plazas throughout the empire *Plazas de la Constitución* (Constitution Squares) and ordering the erection of commemorative monuments. Work to build the St. Augustine monument began the following February. On September 15, 1814, news arrived from Havana of the overthrow of the constitutional government in Spain and restoration of the monarch, Ferdinand VII. By royal decree, destruction of the monuments scattered in towns throughout the Spanish empire began, but St. Augustine's officials refused to tear down what they had sacrificed much to build. St. Augustine's Constitution Monument remains, then, one of the few—perhaps only—such commemorative structures still standing in the New World. Moreover, it is one of the oldest public monuments in the United States. A professionally directed restoration of the masonry obelisk was completed in late 2008. A symbol of the Order of Masons engraved on one of the monument's original tablets reveals the once-pervasive influence of that Protestant-dominated secret order, extending even to what was at the time a Roman Catholic community.

Cathedral-Basilica of St. Augustine

Location
38 Cathedral Place, facing the Plaza, in downtown St. Augustine

Visitor information
The Cathedral-Basilica is an active place of worship. Volunteers conduct tours of the building during normal business hours. A gift store is located within its entrance.

History
The Roman Catholic Parish of St. Augustine is the nation's oldest religious congregation, established in 1565 along with the city itself. Parish records of births, baptisms, and deaths from the sixteenth century survive in its vaults and testify to the early years of America's oldest European settlement. Constructed under the direction of an Irish priest, Father Thomas Hassett, who was educated in Salamanca, Spain, this church building was dedicated on December 8, 1797, during the Second Spanish Period of occupation (1784–1821). Its location on the Plaza near Government House symbolized the importance of the Church in Spanish society. The building's design is reminiscent of eighteenth-century Spanish-American baroque churches, with a facade that sweeps gracefully

upward to a curved parapet surmounted by a gold cross. In 1870, the Diocese of St. Augustine was organized and this building elevated by the Church to the status of a Cathedral, one that serves the bishop of a diocese. A great fire in 1887 destroyed all but the original facade and portions of the building's outside walls. James Renwick— the architect of St. Patrick's Cathedral in New York City, a devout Catholic who spent his winters in St. Augustine—drew the plans for the new church and added to it a magnificent campanile, or bell tower. The building's historical significance earned it designation as a Basilica in 1976.

Exchange Bank Building

Location
24 Cathedral Place, facing the Plaza along its north side

Visitor information
A bank lobby fills the ground floor. The upper floors contain offices.

History
This building—St. Augustine's only "skyscraper," rising six stories—was completed in 1928, in the waning years of the Great Florida Boom. Its Mediterranean features, which include a generous use of terra cotta applied to the masonry exterior finish, typify the architecture of that era. The original owner, the First National Bank of St. Augustine, fell victim to the Great Depression soon after moving into its new offices. Not until 1939, when the Exchange Bank of St. Augustine acquired it, was the building returned to its original use. It has served as a bank ever since. The interior details, complete with massive marble columns that rise some thirty feet to a vaulted ceiling, provide an atmosphere classically associated with an institution of finance. The tall building towers over the Cathedral beside it, a fact that, following the building's completion, prompted municipal officials to adopt an ordinance restricting the height of all new buildings in the city to thirty-five feet. The ordinance, which remained in effect throughout the twentieth century, helped to preserve the architectural scale of the colonial town.

Note the cupola that juts above the crenelated parapet. F. A. Hollingsworth, who designed the building, may have copied this detail from the sentry tower attached to the southeast corner of the Castillo de San Marcos.

Trinity Episcopal Church 1825–1831

Location
South of the Plaza, at the intersection of King Street and St. George Street

Visitor information
Its downtown location makes Trinity Episcopal Church an obvious part of any tour of historic sites and buildings in this part of St. Augustine. Volunteers are generally present on weekdays to provide guided tours of the building.

History
Soon after the formal transfer of Florida to the United States on July 10, 1821, a number of local residents met to "take into consideration the subject of establishing a Protestant Church. . . ." Trinity Church was formally organized on July 2, 1823. Construction of a rectangular building, thirty-six feet by fifty feet, was completed in 1831 and the church consecrated in 1834. The new church occupied the site where, during the British occupation of Florida (1763–1784), the Reverend John Forbes had conducted the first Anglican services in Florida. The chancel was enlarged in 1850. Five decades later, in 1902, a major expansion of the building resulted in the present cruciform shape. The extant parts of the original church include the north porch and tower and the coquina walls of the north transept and baptistery. A Tiffany window, donated in 1905, graces the present St. Peter's Chapel. Among the most notable of the many rectors who served at Trinity Church was the Reverend Benjamin Whipple, who, during a short period of service (1852–1854), extended his ministry to blacks and Native Americans, earning him the designation "Apostle to the Indians." While serving as Bishop of Minnesota in 1862 during the great Sioux uprising in that state, he pleaded with President Abraham Lincoln to commute the death sentences handed to many of the rebellious Indians by a military court.

Bridge of Lions 1927

Location
East of the Plaza in downtown St. Augustine. The bridge, which crosses Matanzas Bay, is part of Florida Highway A1A.

VCB

Visitor information
The bridge is best viewed from the gundeck of the Castillo de San Marcos. The bridge itself contains sidewalks for pedestrians. In the early morning hours, when the sunlight glistens upon the city's buildings, the crown of the bridge affords an excellent position from which to view the bayfront.

History
The Bridge of Lions spans Matanzas Bay (the Intracoastal Waterway) in downtown St. Augustine, linking the mainland portion of the city with its eastern neighborhoods on Anastasia Island. Constructed in 1927, the bridge incorporated features of Mediterranean architecture, which was in vogue at the time and viewed as reflecting Florida's colonial heritage. The bridge, a rare example of an engineering structure displaying a distinct architectural style, draws its name from two marble lions that monitor its western approach. Carved by an Italian sculptor, F. Romanelli, the pair is modeled after the lions that guard the Loggia dei Lanzi in Florence, Italy. Its graceful design and conspicuous location made the bridge one of St. Augustine's most familiar twentieth-century landmarks, viewed by tens of millions of visitors to St. Augustine since its completion. The Bridge of Lions earned listing in the National Register of Historic Places in 1980.

Replacement or restoration? The bridge's deteriorating condition forced the Florida Department of Transportation in 1993 to begin a study of its options with regard to replacing or restoring the bridge. After a decade of public debate, the department decided to restore the historic structure.

Area Two
South of the Plaza

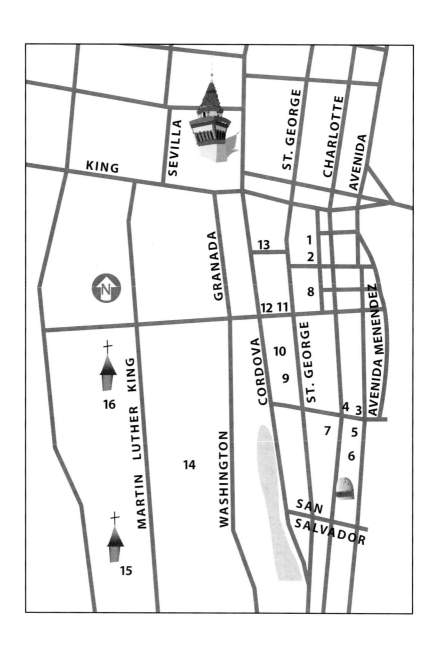

1 Segui–Kirby Smith House   36
2 Ximenez-Fatio House   37
3 González-Alvarez House ("Oldest House")   38
4 Tovar House   39
5 St. Francis Barracks   40
6 National Cemetery   41
7 Fernández-Llambias House   42
8 O'Reilly House   43
9 Col. Upham Cottage   44
10 Bronson Cottage   45
11 Prince Murat House   46
12 Canova House   47
13 Palm Row   48
14 Lincolnville Historic District   49
15 St. Cyprian's Episcopal Church   50
16 St. Benedict the Moor Church   51

Seguí–Kirby Smith House 1788

Location
6 Artillery Lane, at its intersection with Aviles Street, a block south of King Street

Visitor information
The St. Augustine Historical Society's library and collections, located on the second floor of this building, are accessible to the public, free of charge, Tuesday through Friday. The closest parking is found on the streets surrounding the Plaza, one block north of this building.

History

This imposing two-and-a-half-story coquina building provides a good example of Spanish Colonial architecture from the Second Spanish Period (1784–1821). Constructed in 1788, the house played a prominent role in the history of the city, where it has served as a landmark for two centuries. It was the birthplace in 1824 of Lieutenant General Edmund Kirby Smith, a West Point graduate, the highest-ranking Confederate officer from Florida and the last Confederate general to surrender in the Civil War. In 1895, its owners deeded the house in perpetuity to serve as a free public library. For nearly a century, it remained the city's principal library. When St. Johns County constructed a new public library in 1984, the St. Augustine Historical Society assumed responsibility for maintaining the library trust associated with the Seguí–Kirby Smith House and moved its important holdings into the building.

The Congress of the United States permits each of the fifty states to station two statues of historically prominent individuals in the Capitol Building in Washington, D.C. One of Florida's two statues portrays Edmund Kirby Smith.

Ximenez-Fatio House ca. 1798

Location
20 Aviles Street, two blocks south of the Plaza on a narrow brick street, immediately south of the Seguí–Kirby Smith House

Visitor information
The National Society of the Colonial Dames of the state of Florida owns and exhibits the Ximenez-Fatio House. The property is open to visitors on a fee basis from 11:00 A.M. to 4:00 P.M., Monday through Saturday.

History
A Spanish merchant, Andres Ximenez, constructed this building around 1798. His family lived upstairs, while a general store took up the ground floor. Subsequently enlarged, the building became in the nineteenth century one of St. Augustine's most storied places, a fashionable rooming house favored by literary people and artists. One owner, Louisa Fatio, who acquired the house in 1855, played a major role in *Margaret's Story,* a Eugenia Price novel. Louisa Fatio's nephew, Judge David R. Dunham, sold the house to the Florida branch of the Colonial Dames of America in 1939. In the 1980s, that organization undertook a faithful restoration of the building and grounds, which are exhibited as a Florida Territorial Period (1821–1845) house museum.

Shortly after the United States acquired Florida from Spain in 1821, American tourists began showing up in the Ancient City. Heirs to a cultural tradition estranged from the Spanish, the English-speaking Americans regarded St. Augustine as they might a foreign town and delighted in its narrow streets and balconied houses. The Ximenez-Fatio House accurately portrays an early boarding house from that period of St. Augustine's "American discovery."

González-Alvarez House ("Oldest House") ca. 1706

Location
14 St. Francis Street, at the southern end of the Colonial City Historic District

Visitor information
The González-Alvarez House, popularly identified as the "Oldest House," is open to the public seven days a week. The complex of historic buildings and exhibits includes the house museum itself; the Webb Museum, which offers a panorama of St. Augustine history; the Page L. Edwards Jr. Gallery; and the Tovar House. The parking lot for the complex is at the intersection of St. Francis and Charlotte Streets.

History

For over a century, the owners of the González-Alvarez House have portrayed it as the city's oldest house, a claim it once shared with several other St. Augustine buildings. This building, however, has a legitimate case. Its construction in the early years of the eighteenth century, following the destruction of the city in 1702 by invading English forces from the Carolinas, has been carefully documented. The first recorded owner of the building that now stands at this location, Tomás González y Hernández, served as a gunner in an artillery company stationed at the Castillo de San Marcos. Mary Evans Peavett, popularized in a novel by Eugenia Price, owned the house at the time of the American Revolutionary War. Gerónimo Alvarez, a baker who became a leading municipal officer in the early nineteenth century, acquired the property in 1791, and it remained in the Alvarez family for nearly a century. First exhibited as a house museum in 1892, the building was acquired in 1918 by the organization now known as the St. Augustine Historical Society. Since that year, the González-Alvarez House has served as the centerpiece of the Society's museum program. Museum guides weave the building's changes in ownership and appearance into three centuries of local history. This National Historic Landmark is Florida's oldest museum and the state's first house museum.

Tovar House ca. 1763

Location
22 St. Francis Street, next door to the González-Alvarez House ("Oldest House"), at the Charlotte Street intersection

Visitor information

The Tovar House, which is the property of the St. Augustine Historical Society, has historically contained exhibits that are ancillary to the González-Alvarez House or "Oldest House" maintained next door by the Society. A ticket to the Society's museum complex will normally include entry to the Tovar House.

History

José Tovar, a Spanish infantryman, occupied a building on this site in 1763, the year the Spanish Crown transferred ownership of its Florida colony to Great Britain. Gerónimo Alvarez, who lived next door in the González-Alvarez House, purchased the property in 1791. Civil War General Martin G. Hardin (1837–1923), a Union Army veteran who had been befriended as a young man by Abraham Lincoln, resided at this address for about nine years, beginning in 1885. General Hardin extensively remodeled the house to serve as his winter residence and in the process discovered two cannon balls embedded in its walls. That led the general to christen the place the "Casa del Canonaza." The St. Augustine Historical Society acquired the property in 1918, adding the house to its inventory of historical properties.

> The St. Augustine Historical Society, organized in 1883, maintains a research library that serves as the historical archives for St. Augustine and St. Johns County. Because of St. Augustine's primacy in American history, many family names trace their New World origins to the city. Historians and genealogists accordingly make frequent use of the Society's documents and records, which include an extensive collection of maps and art relating to this part of Florida.

St. Francis Barracks ca. 1724–1755

Location
82 Marine Street, along the bayfront at the intersection with St. Francis Street

Visitor information
The St. Francis Barracks contains administrative offices of the Florida National Guard. Visitors may stroll along the sidewalks surrounding the buildings in this area. Parking is absent. A visit to a small military museum within St. Francis Barracks must be scheduled through the Command Historian of the Florida National Guard.

History
The site occupied by St. Francis Barracks has served religious or military purposes since it was first settled by Franciscan missionaries in 1577. For nearly two centuries from its headquarters on this site, the religious order directed an extensive mission system that reached from the Carolinas to what is now Louisiana. The last of the Franciscans left the colony in 1763, when Spain surrendered Florida to Great Britain. The walls of a part of the present building began to rise about 1724, as the friars rebuilt from the destruction caused by the British in 1702.

They completed the work sometime after 1755, not long before the British returned, peacefully, as overseers of the colony. During their twenty-one-year occupation of East Florida, a time that embraced the American Revolutionary War, the British converted the former friary to military use. The building and the area surrounding it have served military purposes ever since. Fire and other types of damage have on several occasions forced rebuilding of the colonial structure. In 1915, the state of Florida obtained the building from the U.S. War Department and made it the headquarters of the Florida National Guard. The building forms the centerpiece of a complex of military buildings whose historical origins span three centuries of St. Augustine's history. The military compound includes one other colonial-era building, the King's Bakery, built by the British, and several splendid residences that date from the late-nineteenth-century Victorian Era.

National Cemetery

Location
Marine Street, on the grounds of the Florida National Guard compound, next to St. Francis Barracks

Visitor information
Sidewalks surround the cemetery and afford visitors a view at any time, but the cemetery grounds are accessible only during posted daylight hours. As with many other locations in this part of the city, parking is scarce.

History
This cemetery, which is Florida's oldest national military burial ground, was authorized by federal legislation in 1881. When the United States gained possession of Florida in 1821, the U.S. Army took over St. Francis Barracks and shortly thereafter set aside land next to it for a post cemetery. The first interment probably occurred in 1828. A large number of early military burials were of soldiers who died on battlefields or of sickness and disease in Florida's Indian wars. Among them are the remains of the 108 men under the command of Major Francis L. Dade, who fell in the first great engagement of the Second Seminole War (1835–1842). Their bodies were brought here from the battlefield near Bushnell, Florida. The three coquina pyramids at the south end of the cemetery cover, in all, the remains of 1,468 Seminole War dead, including the bodies of another fifty-one soldiers who died in that war and had been buried at Picolata at its end. Nearly a century later, in 1930, fifty-one tombstones honoring their memory were planted in a field at Picolata. The stones remain there in a field near the St. Johns River, all but forgotten and overgrown by weeds. Located within the grounds of the Florida National Guard preserve, the St. Augustine National Cemetery is one of ten national cemeteries that displays an illuminated flag twenty-four hours a day.

Fernández-Llambias House ca. 1750

Location
31 St. Francis Street, across from the "Oldest House"

Visitor information
The building is available for social functions through the auspices of the Altrusa Club. It is open to the public on the third Sunday of every month, from 2:00 P.M. to 4:00 P.M. The north or main facade is visible from St. Francis Street. A historical marker stands beneath the north balcony. The St. Augustine Historical Society's parking lot is across the street.

History
One of St. Augustine's few surviving First Spanish Period (1565–1763) buildings, the Fernández-Llambias House began about 1750 as a one-story, two-room, shingle-roofed, coquina-stone residence. Its first recorded owner, Pedro Fernández, sold the house to Jesse Fish in 1764 when Spain relinquished Florida to Great Britain. Fish acted as an agent for many Spanish property owners who abandoned the colony. The house was sold at auction on December 15, 1790, to Mariano Moreno, a sergeant of the Grenadiers. In subsequent years it passed on to a variety of owners, one of whom added the second story and balcony around the turn of the eighteenth century. Catalina Usina Llambias purchased the residence in 1854, and it remained in the Llambias family for the next sixty-five years. Catalina, who died in 1886, was the last person buried in Tolomato Cemetery. The Carnegie Institute, aided by the St. Augustine Historical Society, acquired the property in 1938 and completed restoration of the house in 1954. The Society serves as trustee for the property while the Altrusa Club, an international civic organization, manages the building and spacious grounds.

> The proper name assigned to a historic building is usually associated with the first owner or one who inhabited it over a long period of time, especially if that owner was noteworthy. Some buildings have two historic names assigned to them.

O'Reilly House (ca. 1706)

Location
32 Aviles Street, in the southern part of the Colonial City Historic District

Visitor information
The Sisters of St. Joseph, who have administered the building since 1867, exhibit it as a museum and archives repository.

History
This building holds special fascination because of its First Spanish Period (1565–1763) origin and two-century-long affiliation with the Roman Catholic Church. The building offers a simple architectural plan, typical of an eighteenth-century dwelling. One of a select few houses in St. Augustine that date from the very early years of the eighteenth century, the Father Miguel O'Reilly House ranks as one of the city's oldest buildings. A map prepared in 1764 by a Spanish engineer, J. J. Elixio de la Puente, permits scholars to determine accurately which buildings existed in the city at that time and thus originated during the First Spanish Period. The precise year in which those buildings were constructed remains problematic, however. The presence of certain features, particularly one of the few remaining tabby (a poured mixture of shell, sand, and lime mortar) structural walls in St. Augustine, provides evidence that the O'Reilly House is an early building, rising soon after destruction of the city by English invaders in 1702. The house takes its name from an early owner, Irish priest Father Michael O'Reilly, who served as a chaplain to Spanish troops garrisoned in the town during the Second Spanish Period (1784–1821). Father O'Reilly, who died in 1812, bequeathed the building to a religious order dedicated to education. It has remained in religious use since that time: as a rectory, a school, a convent, a temporary home for retired people, and a museum. The Sisters of St. Joseph supervised a careful restoration of the building in 2001 before opening it for public viewing.

Col. Upham Cottage 1892–1893

Location

268 St. George Street, three blocks south of its intersection with King Street

Visitor information

The building's allure lies in its exuberant architecture, revealing the ornate decorative details commonly associated with the late-nineteenth-century Victorian Period, known in St. Augustine as the Flagler Era (1886–1913). This is a privately owned residence and may be viewed only from the street or sidewalk. No parking is available in the vicinity.

History

One of the most intricately fashioned and colorful of St. Augustine's Victorian "painted ladies," the Upham Cottage displays many features characteristic of the Queen Anne style, popular before the turn of the twentieth century. Elements common to the style of this building include jigsawn rafters and brackets, turned wood posts, and novelty shingles. The porch manifests a Chinese Chippendale appearance, while latticework ornamentation along the gable ends adds to its decorations. The house was built at a time when luxury and elegance were a central part of the lifestyle practiced by St. Augustine's wealthy winter residents. It takes its name from Col. John Upham (1837–1898), a career military officer from Milwaukee and a Civil War veteran who, upon retirement, chose St. Augustine as his place of residence. Col. Upham and his wife, whom he married in 1891, added many touches to the building. Its builder, a local master carpenter named John Ladner, died mysteriously in January 1893, shortly after completing the house. Col. Upham  lived here only five years before his own death. For many decades in the twentieth century, the building served as an apartment house and fell into disrepair. Its modern owners carefully restored the house in the early 1980s.

Bronson Cottage 1876

Location
252 St. George Street, three blocks south of the Plaza

Visitor information
This building is a private residence and may be viewed only from the street or sidewalk. No parking is available in the vicinity.

History

The significance of the Bronson Cottage rests upon the person who designed it, Alexander Jackson Davis (1803–1892), one of the most influential architects in America before the Civil War. Davis designed a number of state capitol buildings, including those in Indiana, Illinois, Ohio, and North Carolina.

His writings and designs helped popularize the Gothic style in the United States and inspired countless "cottages," or country houses, across the central states. "Lyndhurst," perhaps his signature Gothic residence, near Tarrytown, New York, is now owned by the National Trust for Historic Preservation. The Bronson Cottage was, however, a Colonial Revival design, a style that gained favor in 1876 during the centennial observance of the American Revolution. It was one of Davis's last commissions and the only example of his work in Florida, a state he never visited. Davis drew the plans for his friends, Robert D. Bronson and Isabel Donaldson Bronson, winter residents of St. Augustine during the 1870s. Robert Bronson's father, a wealthy New York merchant, was a patron of Davis and financed one of the architect's early publications. From 1960 to 1985, the sisters of St. Joseph used the house as a fine arts academy, before it again became a private residence. The large portico that occupies the front of the building was not a part of the original Davis design, but was added later.

Prince Murat House ca. 1790

Location
248 St. George Street, at the intersection of Bridge Street

Visitor information
The Prince Murat House is part of the Old St. Augustine Village, a museum complex that includes ten historic buildings, whose dates range from 1790 to the late nineteenth century. The Daytona Museum of Arts and Sciences undertook restoration of the ten buildings and creation of the museum complex in 1991. The Old St. Augustine Village museum emphasizes two principal themes: the role of the French in northeast Florida and nineteenth-century American domestic life.

History
The Prince Murat House, constructed about 1790 with the coquina shell stone peculiar to this coastal region, dates to the Second Spanish Period (1784–1821). The house gained its name and its notoriety in St. Augustine historical tradition through its association with Prince Charles Louis Napoleon Achille Murat, a nephew of Napoleon Bonaparte. In 1824, Murat reputedly rented the small house during a short stay in St. Augustine. The following year, he moved to Tallahassee, but from time to time returned to the Ancient City, for he owned several parcels of land along the Matanzas River. On one of his return visits, he met with American poet and philosopher Ralph Waldo Emerson, who also stayed in this house during

a brief sojourn in Florida. Greta Garbo dined here in 1939 at a time when the building contained a restaurant. A steeply pitched roof facing the main facade, extended shed dormers, and a decorative Victorian-era balcony added within the side gable give the house a distinctive flair. Its rose-colored stucco exterior makes the house easy to spot.

Canova House 1840

Location
46 Bridge Street, between Cordova and St. George streets

Visitor information

Like the Prince Murat House (see page 46), the Canova House belongs to the ten-building museum complex known as the Old St. Augustine Village museum. The houses within the museum represent a variety of traditional construction styles and methods extending from the late eighteenth to the early twentieth century. The entrance to the museum is at 143 Cordova Street. A metered municipal parking lot on the west side of Cordova Street offers limited parking. The museum accommodates self-guided and conducted tours.

History

Antonio Canova descended from one of the Minorcan families who came to America in 1767 as a member of an ill-fated attempt by a Scottish entrepreneur, Dr. Andrew Turnbull, to plant a colony at New Smyrna. The colony failed within a decade and in 1777 the survivors fled to St. Augustine. Antonio Canova at one time owned the entire site that now comprises the ten-building Old St. Augustine Village museum complex. He built this house for his son, John, in 1840, during the Territorial Period (1821–1845), five years before Florida entered the Union. It remained in the family throughout most of the nineteenth century. The year before, Canova had built the house next door at 42 Bridge Street for another son, Paul. Now called the Dow House, that building also belongs to the museum complex. The name Canova became familiar to Americans in the 1940s when another family descendant, Judy Canova, won attention as a songstress and comedienne, often appearing with Bob Hope.

Palm Row

Location
One block south of King Street, between Cordova Street and St. George Street

Visitor information
A walking tour of the Plaza area in downtown St. Augustine can easily extend to a stroll along the brick walkway that runs the one-block length of Palm Row. The neighborhood consists of privately owned residential buildings, some of which have been converted to office use.

History
Palm Row is the name attached to a small development containing six residential dwellings that face a palm tree–lined brick walkway one block south of the Plaza. The frame vernacular houses, all of them constructed in 1906 by a local developer, Henry Philip Ammidown, are proportional in size and appearance and offer a picturesque view of late Victorian Era residential architecture. Details found on the buildings, such as jigsawn brackets, bargeboard, and chamfered wood posts, suggest the turn-of-the-century origin of this small neighborhood. Archaeological research conducted in 1978 on one of the lots in Palm Row produced pottery fragments dating to the late 1500s. A map drawn in 1588 shows the location of a house in the vicinity, while later maps of the First Spanish Period (1565–1763) also indicate buildings here. Most likely, this was the site of the first permanent settlement on the west bank of Matanzas Bay (now the Intracoastal Waterway). After abandoning the landing site at what is today the Fountain of Youth Park, the Spanish settlers briefly established themselves on Anastasia Island before returning to the mainland. The residence at 1 Palm Row was in the 1940s the boyhood home of Dr. Michael Gannon, who rose to become a distinguished professor of history at the University of Florida and a leading authority on the history of colonial Florida and St. Augustine.

Lincolnville Historic District Post-1865

Location
The southwestern peninsular section of St. Augustine, west of Cordova Street and south of Bridge Street. Riberia Street, which runs parallel to the San Sebastian River, forms the western boundary of the district.

Visitor information
Essentially a residential neighborhood, this area contains no specific buildings or sites that are presently accessible to visitors.

History
A largely residential neighborhood in St. Augustine's southwest peninsula, this area constitutes the heart of the city's African-American community. Once the site of plantations and orange groves and before that two eighteenth-century Indian mission sites (Pocotalaca and Palaica), Lincolnville emerged after the Civil War as a settlement of freed slaves. First called Africa and later Lincolnville, the neighborhood extended along the western bank of Maria Sanchez Creek. By 1885, the fast-growing community contained churches, schools, and a prosperous black commercial district, surrounded by residences that displayed the flamboyant architecture of the time. African-Americans, whose origins can be traced to the sixteenth-century founding of St. Augustine, played an integral role in the history of the city before the burden of segregation in the late 1800s forced them to create their own community institutions. This fifty-block neighborhood contains the Ancient City's largest collection of Victorian Era buildings. The Frank Butler House (see Butler Beach and Frank Butler Park, page 86) at 87 Washington Street, pictured here, is one example.

Built between 1904 and 1907, it was acquired in 1917 by Butler, a leader in the African-American community who died in 1973. In 1991, the U.S. Department of the Interior listed Lincolnville in the National Register of Historic Places. The marketplace eventually recognized the architectural value of the buildings in Lincolnville, consequently leading to a process of "gentrification" that began to unfold around 1990.

St. Cyprian's Episcopal Church 1900

Location
88 Lovett Street, at the intersection of Lovett Street and Martin Luther King Avenue

Visitor information
The building is easily visible from the sidewalk. Sunday church services begin at 11:00 A.M.

History
The St. Cyprian Episcopal Church is located within the historic African-American neighborhood of Lincolnville. A large diamond-paned window and a gable tower dominate the front facade of this steeply pitched, wood-frame building. It was constructed in 1900 with funds raised by one of St. Augustine's wealthy winter residents, Mrs. Loomis L. White, who felt that the black Episcopalian residents of the city should have a church of their own. In the segregated community of that time, they were denied entry to the traditional white Episcopal church. Mrs. White, the wife of a prominent New York financier, raised the funds largely in Connecticut and in New York. Historical evidence suggests, without certainty, that a New York architect, Howard Hoppin, drew the plans for the building. The frame vernacular building displays elements of the Gothic style that was popularly applied to nineteenth-century churches, especially those belonging to Episcopalian congregations. Wood trusses and dark wood flooring within the interior of the church create an inviting atmosphere for congregants.

St. Benedict the Moor Church 1909

Location
82 Martin Luther King Avenue, six blocks south of its King Street intersection

Visitor Information
This is an active church, with Sunday services. The school building is vacant.

History
Named for the patron saint of blacks in the United States, St. Benedict the Moor Parish is the only African-American Roman Catholic community in St. Augustine. The church, parish rectory, and an abandoned school building stand close to the heart of Lincolnville, the city's historic African-American neighborhood. When Lincolnville began to develop as a settlement of free former slaves after the Civil War, about half of the city's nine hundred blacks professed Roman Catholicism, a relatively high percentage in the largely Protestant South. That number may have resulted from the conversion of escaped slaves to Catholicism during the Spanish Colonial Era, when Catholicism was the only permitted religion. The parish school, built in 1898, was the gift of Mother Katherine Drexel (1858–1955), a wealthy Philadelphia heiress whom Pope John Paul II elevated to sainthood in the year 2000. The order of nuns she founded, the Sisters of the Blessed Sacrament, expressly served "Indians and Colored People,"

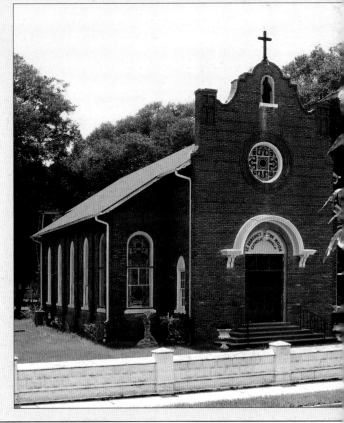

a mission whose purpose gave the white nuns grief in Florida, where state law at the time prohibited racial mixture of any kind in classrooms. From its origins to the time it closed in the mid-1960s, about one hundred students annually enrolled in the St. Benedict school. Before construction of the church building itself, black Catholics worshiped in the segregated east wing of the Cathedral. The bishop of the diocese agreed with parishioners that "they would do better work in the faith" with a building of their own. The church building was completed in 1911 and the bell tower and stained-glass windows were added between 1920 and 1924.

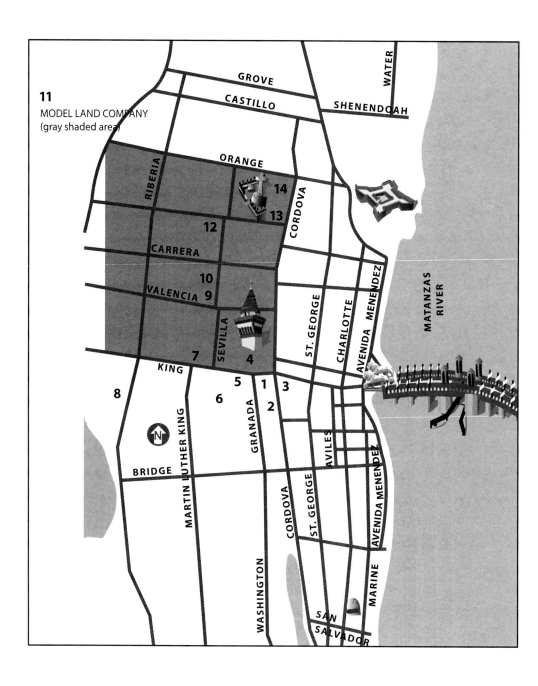

11

MODEL LAND COMPANY
(gray shaded area)

GROVE

CASTILLO

WATER

SHENENDOAH

ORANGE

RIBERIA

14

CORDOVA

13

12

CARRERA

10

VALENCIA 9

SEVILLA

ST. GEORGE

CHARLOTTE

AVENIDA MENENDEZ

MATANZAS RIVER

7

4

KING

5

1

3

8

6

2

MARTIN LUTHER KING

GRANADA

AVILES

AVENIDA MENENDEZ

N

BRIDGE

CORDOVA

ST. GEORGE

MARINE

WASHINGTON

SAN SALVADOR

1 Alcazar Hotel (City Hall)   54

2 Lightner Museum   55

3 Casa Monica Hotel   56

4 Ponce de Leon Hotel (Flagler College)   57

5 Villa Zorayda (Zorayda Castle)   58

6 Xavier Lopez House   59

7 Markland   60

8 Solla-Carcaba Cigar Factory   61

9 Flagler Memorial Presbyterian Church   62

10 Ingraham House (Presbyterian Manse)   63

11 Model Land Company Historic District   64

12 Ancient City Baptist Church   65

13 Grace United Methodist Church   66

14 Tolomato Cemetery   67

Alcazar Hotel 1888

Location
5 King Street, on the southwest corner of the King Street and Cordova Street intersection

Visitor information
The Alcazar faces north upon a large open courtyard, which is dominated by a bronze statue of the city's founder, Pedro Menéndez de Avilés, a gift to St. Augustine from the people of Avilés, Spain.

History
The second of the great hotels in St. Augustine constructed by Henry Flagler in his attempt to create a southern resort city, the Alcazar Hotel was, like its predecessor the Ponce de Leon Hotel, designed by the nationally prominent architectural firm of Carrere and Hastings. Terra cotta ornamentation decorates the walls and rooflines of the massive, poured concrete structure, cast in the Moorish Revival style. The building

originally contained a large indoor swimming pool, the first such facility in Florida. Conceived by Flagler as a lower cost annex to the Ponce de Leon Hotel, the Alcazar closed its doors in 1931, only four decades after its completion. Chicago industrialist Otto Lightner purchased the abandoned building in 1946 for $150,000 and donated it to the City of St. Augustine with the understanding that it would forever house his museum of collectibles (see Lightner Museum). In 1972, the city moved its offices into the Alcazar, which it continues to share with the Lightner Museum.

A former partner of John D. Rockefeller in the Standard Oil Company, Henry Flagler retired to St. Augustine in 1886, but quickly plunged into business again as a railroad and hotel entrepreneur. He set about converting the small town into the "Newport of the South," a vacation destination for wealthy Northerners and potential patrons of his railroad. Within a decade, however, Flagler began extending his rail line southward along the east coast of Florida to warmer parts of the peninsula.

Lightner Museum 1948

Location
5 King Street, the same address as the Alcazar Hotel. The Lightner Museum occupies the extended south wing of the building

Visitor information
The museum shares the Alcazar Hotel with the municipal government of St. Augustine. The entrance to the museum is located within the south quadrant of the interior courtyard. Open on a daily basis, the Lightner displays its collections on three floors. The museum has changing exhibits in its Transition Gallery. Particularly fascinating is a group of mechanical musical instruments (player pianos) whose melodies resound throughout the museum twice each day.

History
Founded in 1948, the Lightner Museum holds a variety of collections that were primarily gathered in his lifetime by wealthy Chicago industrialist Otto Lightner. Born in Wichita, Kansas, in 1887, Lightner made his fortune in the publishing trade. His magazine for collectors, first issued in 1931, proved instantly successful and continued to thrive during the Great Depression. He took his own advice to heart and acquired collectibles at fire sale prices throughout the 1930s. The cavernous, empty Alcazar, set in a tourist city that the self-styled "King of Hobbies" enjoyed visiting, offered a fitting repository for his collections. Lightner died in 1950 and lies buried beneath a large monument in the courtyard of the Alcazar. Designed to appeal to the curiosity of all ages, the Lightner Museum's unique offerings include natural history, fine arts, mechanical musical instruments, ceramics, glass, toys, furniture, and thousands of other unusual objects. If the collection has a temporal focus, it is the Victorian Era. Few such collections exceed it in quality.

VCB

Casa Monica Hotel 1888

Location
95 Cordova Street, at the intersection of Cordova and King Streets, in the heart of downtown St. Augustine

Visitor information
The Casa Monica Hotel operates as a full-service hotel.

History
Designed and built by Franklin W. Smith, a Boston architectural critic and businessman, the Casa Monica Hotel first opened in January 1888. One of three massive Flagler Era buildings constructed of poured concrete, the Casa Monica was designed in the Moorish Revival style, introduced to St. Augustine by Smith for his residence, the Villa Zorayda, which is located one block west of this hotel. Soon after the Casa Monica was completed, entrepreneur Henry Flagler purchased the building, renamed it the Cordova Hotel, and added it to his collection of hotels as an annex to the Alcazar Hotel, on the west side of Cordova Street. An enclosed walkway spanning Cordova Street once connected the two hotels. In 1961 the Florida East Coast Railway Company sold the building to the St. Johns County Board of County Commissioners for use as the county courthouse. After using it for thirty-five years, the County Commission abandoned the building in 1995 when it moved the courthouse offices to new facilities several miles north of the city. Richard Kessler, an Orlando hotel entrepreneur, restored the original use and historic splendor of the great building just in time for the new millennium, invoking a renewed era of magnificent hostelry in St. Augustine.

Ponce de Leon Hotel (Flagler college) 1888

Location
74 King Street, at the intersection of King and Cordova streets

Visitor information
The building occupies an oversized block of land surrounded by streets and sidewalks that are accessible to visitors. It provides administrative offices, classrooms, and student housing for Flagler College, a four-year school of higher education. Two major interior rooms may be viewed at scheduled times, but only on a guided tour. The entrance for such visits is from the King Street side of the building, behind the statue of Henry Flagler.

History
The first of the great St. Augustine hotels constructed by railroad entrepreneur Henry Flagler, who intended to refashion the city as a Southern resort for wealthy Northerners, the Ponce de Leon inaugurated a brief period of opulent architecture that began and ended in the closing years of the nineteenth century. Flagler commissioned a pair of young architects, Thomas Hastings and John

M. Carrere, to create his building. The two had been working for the great New York architectural firm of McKim, Mead and White. They drew from a variety of Mediterranean precedents to fashion the Ponce de Leon, creating a style of architecture that influenced design throughout Florida for the next half-century. Another young architect, Bernard Maybeck, who later won national prominence in California, designed the interior spaces, evoking the Victorian splendor of America's Gilded Age. Louis Comfort Tiffany, who had only a short time before reorganized his company to specialize in glass for builders, contributed stained-glass art to the building's interior. His contributions to the Ponce de Leon helped to make his reputation. The Ponce de Leon served as a hotel for well over half a century before it was converted for educational use and renamed Flagler College in 1968.

Villa Zorayda (Zorayda Castle) 1883

Location
83 King Street, facing the Ponce de Leon Hotel (Flagler College)

Visitor information
The building's flamboyant architecture is easily viewed from King Street. In early 2008, the building was reopened to the public as a museum displaying artifacts associated with its origins.

History
Historically named the Villa Zorayda, the Zorayda Castle, as it is more popularly known, offers St. Augustine's earliest example of the Moorish Revival style. Conceived by Franklin W. Smith, a friend of railroad and hotel entrepreneur Henry Flagler, the Villa Zorayda, built for Smith as his winter residence and completed in 1883, was the first edifice in St. Augustine constructed of poured concrete. Flagler and his architects emulated Smith's construction methods and stylistic philosophy in planning the great hotels and churches they undertook to build throughout the city. Like the Villa Zorayda, the Ponce de Leon Hotel, completed five years later, employed poured concrete wall construction with a limited use of iron reinforcement. Its architectural integrity carefully preserved, Zorayda Castle remained open on exhibit for more than half a century before it closed to the public in 1998 for remodeling. A close student of Spanish history and architecture, Franklin Smith introduced the revival in St. Augustine of stylistic forms that reflected the city's Iberian heritage. The extent to which he may have influenced his friend, Henry Flagler, to follow his lead remains a historical uncertainty. The eclectic style that resulted, which Florida architectural historians call "Mediterranean Revival," stamped its character on many cities in Florida, most notably Boca Raton, Palm Beach, and Coral Gables.

Xavier Lopez House 1903

Location
93-1/2 King Street, in back of the parking lot of the city's Main Post Office, on the west side of Zorayda Castle

Visitor information
Upon its restoration in 1980, the house was placed in commercial use. Parking is not available in its immediate vicinity.

History
Constructed in 1903 by the noteworthy St. Augustine contracting firm of William Fishwick and K. McKinnon, the Xavier Lopez House originally served as the residence of a prominent St. Augustine businessman, whose name remains historically attached to the building. The Xavier Lopez House offers an example of the Queen Anne style, a popular residential design of the late nineteenth century that featured sweeping verandas, towers, and decorative "gingerbread" wood trim applied to a highly articulated floor plan. Xavier Lopez managed the Surprise Store on Cathedral Street for many years and held a number of local political offices. Once common to St. Augustine, few Queen Anne buildings remain in the city, and none more tastefully preserved than the Xavier Lopez House. Faced with destruction in 1980 when the adjacent U.S. Post Office expanded its parking lot, the house was purchased by a local entrepreneur, moved from King Street to its present location, and carefully restored to its original appearance. It gained listing in the National Register of Historic Places in 1993.

A second house on the same lot served for many years as the winter home of Dr. John Harvey Kellogg (1852–1943), the inventor of breakfast cereal, health food advocate, and founder of the Kellogg Cereal Company. The "Kellogg House" (Kellogg never owned it) was unfortunately demolished in 1980 to make way for a U.S. Post Office parking lot.

Markland

Location
102 King Street, one block west of the historic Ponce de Leon Hotel (Flagler College)

Visitor information
King Street provides the best view of the building's main facade. Markland, used administratively by Flagler College, is not open to the public. There is no parking in the vicinity. Visitors must remain on the sidewalk when viewing the building.

History
Markland offers an outstanding example of the Greek Revival style that was favored as a residential design by many wealthy Americans in the pre–Civil War era, especially in Southern states. It was built for Dr. Andrew Anderson, a prominent nineteenth-century civic leader. When its construction began in 1839, the residence occupied the center of one of Florida's most famous orange groves. Anderson's son, also Dr. Andrew Anderson (1839–1924), sold a portion of the grove to his friend, railroad entrepreneur and hotel builder Henry Flagler. Upon that piece of land, Flagler built the great Ponce de Leon Hotel, completed in 1888 and situated immediately east of this building. In 1900, the younger Anderson enlarged Markland to its present stately appearance. Flagler College acquired the property in 1968.

An outstanding civic benefactor, the younger Dr. Andrew Anderson in 1923 contributed to the City of St. Augustine a life-size statue of Florida's European discoverer, Ponce de Leon, which stands high atop a large granite pedestal east of the Plaza. It is an exact replica of the original piece at Ponce de Leon's tomb in San Juan, Puerto Rico. Dr. Anderson also donated to the city the two marble lions that monitor the western end of the Bridge of Lions and that gave the famous bridge its name.

Solla-Carcaba Cigar Factory 1909

Location
88 Riberia Street, one block south of the intersection of Riberia Street and King Street

Visitor information
The Solla-Carcaba Cigar Factory is a privately owned, commercial office building. The interior has been altered to serve modern uses, but the exterior closely reflects the building's original appearance.

History

The Solla-Carcaba Cigar Factory, completed in 1909, is the last remnant of the cigar industry in St. Augustine, one whose origins in the Ancient City date to the early part of the nineteenth century. P. F. Carcaba, a native of Oviedo, Spain, brought his cigar-making business from Cincinnati to St. Augustine in 1893 and began the manufacture of pure Havana "Caballeros," whose boxes featured pictures of Henry Flagler's great hotels. After Carcaba's death in 1906, his son, W. H. Carcaba, partnered with his brother-in-law, Agustine Solla, to raise public money and build a new factory. Fred A. Henderich, a pioneer in restoration architecture who redesigned much of St. Augustine after the great 1914 fire, drew the plans for the building. The Carcaba company failed in 1917. The Pamies-Arango Cigar Company, which had been operating out of a smaller building in the city, purchased its assets and remained in business until the collapse of the Florida economy in 1926. A succession of owners and businesses subsequently inhabited St. Augustine's oldest surviving major industrial building before its restoration in 1985.

When revolutionary chaos engulfed Spanish-controlled Cuba after 1868, many of the island's cigar manufacturers and the workers who hand-rolled the tobacco fled to Florida. The industry remained profitable until the 1920s, when smokers, joined by a growing number of women, turned to cigarettes.

Flagler Memorial Presbyterian Church

Location

36 Valencia Street, at the intersection with Sevilla Street, diagonally across the grounds of the Ponce de Leon Hotel (Flagler College)

Visitor information

A guide is available seven days a week during normal business hours to explain the history and architecture of the building. Church services are held on Sunday mornings. There is no parking in the immediate vicinity.

History

Another legacy of the Flagler Era (1886–1913) in St. Augustine's history, the Flagler Memorial Presbyterian Church offers a classic example of the Venetian Renaissance style. The building, designed by nationally renowned architects Thomas Hastings and John Carrere, was financed by hotel entrepreneur Henry Flagler in memory of his daughter, Jennie Louise, who died tragically in 1889 at the age of thirty-four. The remains of Flagler and his first wife, Mary, lie beside those of his daughter in a mausoleum within the church. Shaped in the form of a Latin Cross, the building was patterned after St. Mark's Cathedral in Venice. Within its interior, twenty-four arches supported by terra cotta pillars reach upward from the center of the cruciform structure to support the Venetian-style copper dome, which stands 150 feet above the floor. Elaborate capitals of old gold and white terra cotta decorate the base of the dome. The stained-glass windows, designed by Herman T. Schladermundt, were added in 1901 and depict religious themes. Formed in 1824 with twelve charter members and two elders, this was Florida's first Presbyterian congregation.

Ingraham House (Presbyterian Manse) 1894

Location
32 Sevilla Street, on the north side of Flagler Memorial Presbyterian Church

Visitor information
The manse is a private dwelling and not accessible to the public.

History
Historically known as the Ingraham House, the Presbyterian Manse serves as the residence for the pastor of Flagler Memorial Presbyterian Church. Henry Flagler, whose interests owned the Ponce de Leon Hotel, had this residence built for James E. Ingraham, president of Flagler's Model Land Company and vice president of his Florida East Coast Railway. Ingraham was also associated in business with Gen. Henry Sanford and Henry B. Plant, developers like Flagler who were engaged, respectively, in promoting growth within the central and western parts of the peninsula. In 1892, Ingraham led a small expedition across the Everglades, trekking from Fort Myers to Miami through an uncharted vastness of water, muck, and sawgrass—the first persons known to have made the treacherous journey. Upon Ingraham's death in 1924, the heirs to Flagler's interests donated the building to the Presbyterian Church for use as a residential manse. A Colonial Revival–style building decorated with classical features, the stately residence's beauty is found in such ornamental details as wood columns, spindle work, and fanlight windows. Three highly articulated dormers pierce the east slope of its hip roof.

Model Land Company Historic District 1839–1930

Location

The district's boundaries include King Street to the south, Cordova Street on the east, Orange Street along the north, and Ponce de Leon Boulevard to the west. Two easily identifiable large structures mark the district's southern corners: the Ponce de Leon Hotel, now Flagler College, at its southeastern tip, and the former Florida East Coast Railway headquarters (now the property of Flagler College and shown here) at its southwestern corner.

Visitor information

The Model Land Company Historic District includes a large residential neighborhood, commercial buildings, and much of the campus of Flagler College. While touring this area, visitors should walk or employ a tourist vehicle—either a carriage or train—because of the limited parking within the neighborhood. Visitors may observe the interiors of the Ponce de Leon Hotel (Flagler College), the Flagler Memorial Presbyterian Church, and Grace Methodist Church on sponsored tours.

History

Entrepreneur Henry Flagler was not content with merely building world-class hotels when, in the 1880s, he set out to refashion St. Augustine as a Southern resort city.

He also undertook the development of an approximately forty-acre residential neighborhood north and west of his flagship Ponce de Leon Hotel, thirty-seven acres of which he personally acquired. He underwrote the construction of three well-designed churches within two blocks of the hotel and constructed his winter home, "Kirkside," next to one of them—the Flagler Memorial Presbyterian Church, which contains his burial vault (Kirkside was demolished in 1955). The sale of lots and construction of homes within the neighborhood proceeded slowly for three decades. The buildings within the Model Land Company Historic District offer a diverse range of styles, from ones typically associated with the architecture of the Victorian Era to Mediterranean Revival types characteristic of the 1920s Boom Period. Flagler named the streets in the subdivision for cities in Spain, a tribute to St. Augustine's heritage.

Ancient City Baptist Church 1895

Location

30 Carrera Street, within the heart of the Model Land Company Historic District, one block north of Flagler Memorial Presbyterian Church

Visitor information

Since this is an active church, interior access is generally permitted only during hours of worship. The city's main parking facility is just two blocks north of this site.

History

A cone-shaped roof atop a round three-story tower and a smaller, matching turret on the opposite side of the building suggest the Romanesque Revival style of this late-nineteenth-century church. Decorative brickwork adds to the Romanesque effect of the building. It rests in the most architecturally impressive part of the Model Land Company subdivision that Henry Flagler organized upon completing construction of the great Ponce de Leon Hotel in 1888. He donated the property on which this building rests to the Baptist congregation on the condition that it construct a church exceeding $10,000 in cost. The building cost $15,000.

Based upon Roman classical design, the Romanesque architectural style first appeared in eleventh- and twelfth-century Europe. Its characteristics include massively thick masonry walls, round arches, and towers. Popularly associated in the United States with the work of architect Henry Hobson Richardson (1838–1886), the style quickly swept the country in the 1880s and was widely applied to large public buildings such as courthouses, churches, and railroad stations.

Grace United Methodist Church 1887–1888

Location

8 Carrera Street, at the northwest corner of the intersection of Cordova Street and Carrera Street

Visitor information

The church is an active house of worship. Volunteers are generally on duty during daylight hours to provide guided tours of select parts of the church. One room in the building, accessible to visitors, contains photographs and documents relating to the history of the building.

History

The Grace United Methodist Church belongs to the complex of massive structures that serve as a direct legacy to the architectural contributions of entrepreneur Henry Flagler to St. Augustine. In exchange for property the congregation owned, and which Flagler needed for one of his hotels, he donated the money to build this church. His architects, John M. Carrere and Thomas Hastings, executed the design in a Spanish Renaissance Revival style, employing both a generous use of terra cotta ornamentation and the poured concrete structural system the architects had used in building the Alcazar and Ponce de Leon hotels. Begun in 1887, the Grace United Methodist Church was completed a year later. Within a distance of two blocks also stand the Flagler Memorial Presbyterian Church and the Ancient City Baptist Church, like this building the result of Henry Flagler's generosity.

"Terra cotta" is Italian for "baked earth," and refers to select red clays molded into ornamental blocks and used to decorate the interiors and exteriors of buildings. In the United States, terra cotta enjoyed popularity as a building material for about a century, beginning in the mid-1800s. An ancient building material, it was introduced to Spain during the Moorish occupation of the Iberian Peninsula (752–1492).

Tolomato Cemetery ca. 1750 to 1884

Location
The west side of Cordova Street, half a block south of its intersection with Orange Street

Visitor information
A secure fence surrounds the cemetery, which is visible from the sidewalk along Cordova Street. The cemetery is closed to the public. The city's main parking facility at the Visitor Information Center is a block north of this cemetery.

History
Once the site of an Indian village, this plot of land became a burial place for Christian Indians late in the First Spanish Period (1565–1763). Interment of Catholics in this cemetery may have begun during the British Period (1763–1784) with arrival of the Minorcans in St. Augustine. The cemetery was closed for burials in 1884. The mortuary chapel on the grounds contains the remains of the Most Reverend Jean Pierre Augustin Marcellin Verot, the first bishop of St. Augustine, who died in 1876. The tombstones within the Tolomato Cemetery reflect the names of many families closely associated with the city's history, as do other cemeteries in St. Augustine. For a time, this cemetery also held the tomb of Father Felix Varela, a Cuban priest and intellectual leader, who died in St. Augustine in 1853. His body was later transferred to Cuba, though his crypt still stands in the Tolomato Cemetery.

In 1859, Bishop Verot established the city's convent school, predecessor of the present St. Joseph's Academy. In the post–Civil War Era, he championed educational opportunities for freed slaves.

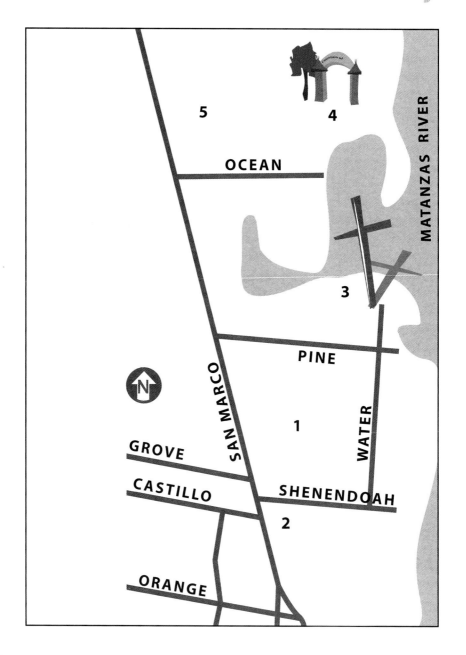

5

4

MATANZAS RIVER

OCEAN

3

PINE

N

1

WATER

SAN MARCO

GROVE

CASTILLO

SHENENDOAH

2

ORANGE

1 Abbott Tract Historic District   70
2 Warden Castle (Ripley's "Believe It
    or Not!" Museum) 71
3 Mission of Nombre de Dios   72
4 Fountain of Youth Park 73
5 The Old Jail   74

Abbott Tract Historic District 1842–1930

Location

The Abbott Tract Historic District takes up about twelve city blocks between San Marco Avenue and Matanzas Bay and begins at the north edge of the Castillo de San Marcos property. The Mission of Nombre de Dios marks the northern boundary of the district.

Visitor information

Once an exclusively residential neighborhood, the district has given way to some commercial use, which is presently restricted to the buildings along its western edge, facing San Marco Avenue. The narrow streets in this neighborhood reflect a time before the automobile became the popular mode of transportation.

History

The Abbott Tract Historic District occupies a parcel of land lying between the original 1565 settlement site and the Castillo de San Marcos, constructed in the late 1600s. Spanish authorities prohibited any interruption in the landscape north of the Castillo in order to maintain an artillery "field of fire" (called the *mil y quinientas* or "fifteen hundred"), which in Spanish *varas* was the prescribed distance

of the clearing (about 4,500 feet). The land remained in agricultural use until 1839, when Peter Sken Smith of Philadelphia filed a subdivision plat for parcels along the river and began selling lots. Only about twelve houses were erected there before the Civil War, but in the 1870s as St. Augustine began expanding outside of the old city, building in the neighborhood took off, continuing at a steady pace into the early years of the twentieth century. The tract takes its name from Lucy Abbott, a woman who spearheaded development in this part of the city after the Civil War. Her residence, located in this district, is pictured here. The neighborhood still contains many fine examples of Victorian Era architecture, though the styles found throughout the district reflect the city's architectural growth through the 1920s Boom Period. Water Street, running along the river marsh, was St. Augustine's preferred address for many decades. The neighborhood won listing in the National Register of Historic Places in 1983.

Warden Castle
(Ripley's "Believe It or Not!" Museum) 1887

Location

19 San Marco Avenue, at its intersection with Castillo Drive, north of the grounds surrounding the Castillo de San Marcos and across the street from the Visitor Information Center

Visitor information

The museum within the building is open daily. Parking is available on the grounds and at the Visitor Information Center parking facility.

History

William G. Warden, a Standard Oil Company partner of Henry Flagler and John D. Rockefeller, constructed this building as his residence in 1887. Although not associated with Flagler's St. Augustine enterprises, Warden became financially involved in the city's development through the St. Augustine Improvement Company, which he owned. Warden Castle reflects in its detailing the Moorish Revival style of architecture, like the Villa Zorayda, built four years earlier. For seven centuries the Moors occupied most of the Iberian peninsula and left their imprint on the architecture and language of Spain. The roofline of Warden Castle is topped with battlements and massive chimneys. The loggia was added at the

VCB

turn of the century. The building and its elaborate interior reflect the exuberance of the Gilded Age and St. Augustine's place as a resort city. Hotelier Norton Baskin and his wife, Pulitzer Prize–winning author Marjorie Kinnan Rawlings, purchased the building in 1941, the year in which they were married. The pair lived in a top-floor apartment and maintained a twenty-five-room hotel in the floors below. Rawlings, by then a well-known author, attracted many leading literary figures to her hotel. One of them was Robert Ripley, whose "Believe It or Not!" cartoons were a staple part of newspaper "funny pages." In 1950, Ripley purchased the building from Baskin and created within it the first of what has become an empire of museums.

Mission of Nombre de Dios 1565–1821

Location

The west bank of Matanzas Bay, north of the Abbott Tract Historic District

Visitor information

The site, marked by a towering rust-colored cross visible from most parts of the city and maintained by the Catholic Diocese of St. Augustine, includes a small chapel and cemetery accessible seven days a week during normal business hours. A parking lot next to the modern church on San Marco Avenue accommodates vehicles at no cost. North of the parking lot is a gift store and information counter.

History

Mission settlements constituted a highly significant part of Spain's colonial presence in Florida. One of the earliest, the Mission of Nombre de Dios ("Name of God"), was established not long after the settlement of St. Augustine. This site, still in religious use today, contains an early cemetery. It is near the location where Pedro Menéndez de Avilés first stepped ashore

in 1565. Here, close to a large Indian village named Seloy, the Spanish planted their original community and Spanish priests conducted the first religious services for what became the parish of St. Augustine. The tall, stainless steel cross marking the mission's location was erected in 1965 to commemorate the St. Augustine Quadricentennial, the four hundredth anniversary of the city's founding. Weighing seventy tons and reaching 208 feet into the sky, it is the tallest cross in the Western Hemisphere. Near the cross and at the foot of a small bridge leading to it stands a statue of the chaplain who accompanied the 1565 Menéndez expedition, Father Francisco López de Mendoza Grajales, who celebrated here the first Mass, or church service, in the new colony. A chapel on the grounds, dedicated to Mary as the Patroness of Motherhood, a devotion brought from Spain in 1603, is a 1918 reconstruction on the foundations of the 1615 building that suffered repeated destruction by war, pirates, and hurricanes.

Fountain of Youth Park Late 1500s

Location

155 Magnolia Avenue, along a street that runs beneath a canopy of trees that affords one of the city's most scenic vistas

Visitor information

Privately owned, the Fountain of Youth Park is maintained as a public attraction and is accessible to visitors on a daily admission basis. Ample parking is available on the premises.

History

For nearly a century, this site has been portrayed as the landing place of Juan Ponce de León, the first governor of both Puerto Rico and Florida, the first recorded European to set foot upon Florida, and the explorer who gave the state its name. Ponce de León sailed from Puerto Rico with three ships on a mission of exploration, landing about the time of Easter somewhere along the east coast of Florida in April, 1513. He named the land "Florida" after the Castilian name for Easter, *Pascua Florida*, a term with connotations relating to the flowering of plants in springtime. His orders from King Ferdinand of Spain listed powerful motives for finding new lands in a hitherto uncharted region. Searching for the fabled Fountain of Youth was not among them. Recent scholarship places the landing site farther to the south, around the area of Cape Canaveral. It was almost certainly not St. Augustine. Still, this site is important in other ways. It was the location of a large pre-1565 Timucuan Indian village and the landing site for the colonizing expedition from Spain led by Admiral Pedro Menéndez de Aviléz that came ashore on September 8, 1565. In the 1990s, archaeological excavations at the park revealed the presence of the first Spanish fortification and settlement in St. Augustine, which established

the town as the oldest permanently occupied community of European origin in the United States of America. The presence of the Fountain of Youth Park on this site, throughout a century of modern development, has served to prevent the destruction of historic and archaeological resources of national and international significance.

The Old Jail 1891

Location
167 San Marco Avenue, close to a half-mile north of the Castillo de San Marcos

Visitor information
The Old Jail forms part of a complex of buildings that support a city tourist trolley business. The building is accessible to the public for an admission fee. The complex includes a small museum, restaurant, and gift store. Parking is available at the site.

History
Constructed in 1891 by the P.J. Pauley Jail Building and Manufacturing Company, an internationally recognized builder of prison facilities from St. Louis, Missouri, this structure is significant for its architectural design and its history. The two-and-one-half-story Romanesque Revival–style building served as the county jail from that year until 1953, when the St. Johns County Board of County Commissioners abandoned the facility and sold it to a local entrepreneur, Henry L. "Slim" McDaniel. He converted the building into a tourist attraction and named it "Old Jail." The building's immediate adaptation to a pubic attraction thus afforded visitors a rare view of a virtually unaltered nineteenth-century penal institution. The building was carefully rehabilitated in 1993 and, at that time, listed in the National Register of Historic Places. Its original construction was funded, in part, by railroad and hotel magnate Henry Flagler, who wanted the then-existing county jail removed from its location near his newly built Ponce de Leon Hotel, after a grand jury declared the facility a public nuisance. Flagler offered the Board of County Commissioners $10,000 to build a new jail somewhere else. The Board selected a site in what was then the north part of the city, about a mile from Flagler's hotel. As for the "public nuisance" jail facility, Flagler purchased that building from the Board of County Commissioners and promptly ordered it demolished. In its place, he built the Bacchus Club, Florida's first plush gambling casino. The casino building is no longer standing, replaced about half a century ago by a modern bank building.

The Old Jail

Area Five
Anastasia Island

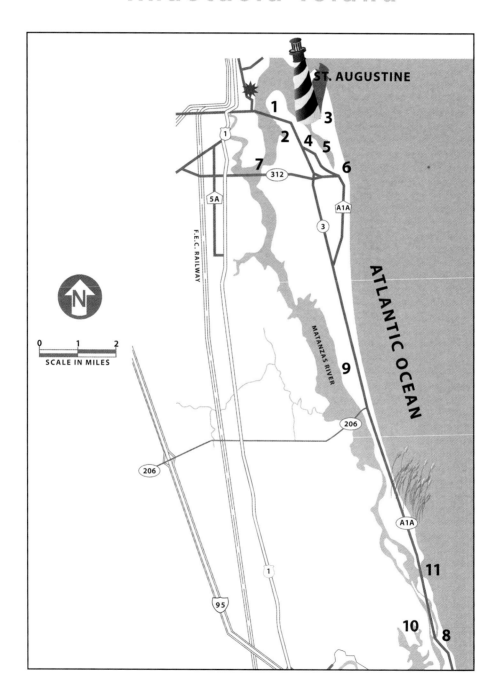

1 Oglethorpe Battery Park   78

2 St. Augustine Alligator Farm   79

3 St. Augustine Lighthouse
   and Keeper's Quarters   80

4 Old Spanish Well and Chimney   81

5 Old Spanish Quarries   82

6 Anastasia State Recreation Area   83

7 Fish Island Site   84

8 Summer Haven   85

9 Butler Beach and Frank Butler Park   86

10 Fort Matanzas National Monument   87

11 Massacre of the French, Matanzas Inlet   88

Location

Cross the Bridge of Lions and head south along Anastasia Boulevard to Arredondo Street and then north to Zorayda Street.

Visitor information

The City of St. Augustine maintains the park, a half-block grass lot, which features a stone monument commemorating the historic event that occurred here. Parking is available on the surrounding streets. Although modern development obstructs a view of the Castillo de San Marcos from this location, visitors can gain an impression of the distance over which British artillery hurled shells at the fortress in 1740.

History

From this site, British troops led by General James Oglethorpe, Governor of the Colony of Georgia and commander of the Georgia and Carolina militia, bombarded the Castillo de San Marcos with cannon shot for nearly a month, from June 27 to July 20, 1740. The Castillo's massive coquina walls absorbed the cannon balls and the fortress suffered only minor damage. The Spanish commander, Governor Manuel de Montiano, ordered return fire, though the artillery exchange proved indecisive

to the battle. Provisions arrived from Havana just in time to relieve a critical shortage of food and supplies within the Castillo. The Spanish defenders could not have held on much longer, but Oglethorpe did not know that. Frustrated by the stalemate and concerned about the oncoming hurricane season, he ordered a withdrawal to Georgia, ending a second failed attempt by British arms in the early eighteenth century to take the great fortress.

Representatives of three states whose colonial militia fought in the 1740 engagement—South Carolina, Georgia, and Florida—helped dedicate the Oglethorpe Battery Monument on March 20, 1938. The ceremony attracted hundreds of spectators caught up in the spirit of restoration that was then beginning to grip the Ancient City.

St. Augustine Alligator Farm 1893

Location

999 Anastasia Boulevard, A1A South, on Anastasia Island, approximately one mile east of the Bridge of Lions

Visitor information

This attraction is open daily to the public for an admission fee, with parking available at the location. It contains the most extensive collection of alligators and crocodiles in the world, along with many other reptiles, animals, and birds. A saltwater crocodile from New Guinea named "Maximo," the largest captive reptile in North America, was added to the collection in 2003, and a Komodo dragon was added in 2008.

History

The St. Augustine Alligator Farm is one of the oldest continuously operated attractions in Florida. Its origins date to the early 1890s, a time when St. Augustine was emerging as a national tourist destination. Public fascination with alligators held in a pen near a small hotel at St. Augustine Beach, about three miles south of the city proper, led the owners to create a small zoological park. A familiar local landmark by the 1920s, the St. Augustine Alligator Farm's reputation spread throughout the country in the 1940s, when thousands of servicemen stationed in the area during World War II visited the facility and later helped to broadcast its popularity. The building that presently contains the entrance and gift shop was constructed in 1937, following a fire that destroyed the attraction's previous quarters. Although it is primarily a zoological attraction, the Alligator Farm also cooperates in significant research on reptiles and other animals through an association with the University of Florida and major national zoological institutions. The Alligator Farm's role in the development of Florida tourism was recognized in 1993 by its listing in the National Register of Historic Places. The St. Augustine Alligator Farm has also earned national accreditation by the American Zoological Association.

St. Augustine Lighthouse and Keeper's Quarters 1871–1876

Location

Anastasia Island, three blocks north of A1A, one mile south of the Bridge of Lions

Visitor information

The St. Augustine Lighthouse & Museum, Inc., operates a full-service museum at this location, with exhibits and a gift store. Visitors can walk the winding stairs to the top of the tower. There is an admission fee. Few lighthouse exhibits in the nation exceed the quality of this one.

History

One of the city's most familiar landmarks, the St. Augustine Lighthouse was one of a series of lighthouses constructed along the Atlantic coastline during the nineteenth century. The northern tip of Anastasia Island, where the existing tower is located, has been closely associated with the defense and maritime history of St. Augustine since the sixteenth century, when Spanish officials erected a sentry tower overlooking the water approaches to the city in the vicinity of what is now Lighthouse Park. About a century later, the Spanish constructed a guardhouse and lookout tower at the site. In 1763, under British control, the tower was raised and a cannon placed atop it to signal the approach of vessels. After the United States took possession of Florida in 1821, federal authorities converted the Spanish watchtower to a lighthouse. Located on a steadily eroding shoreline, the old lighthouse was eventually undermined by the ocean and washed into the sea on August 22, 1880. The present lighthouse was completed in 1874 and the Keeper's Quarters, a picturesque two-story brick residence set within a grove of shade trees, finished in 1876. Nearly destroyed by fire in 1970, it was restored a decade later through local efforts. The U.S. Coast Guard gave the St. Augustine Lighthouse & Museum, Inc., title to the property in 2003, the first of a projected series of such conveyances throughout the nation.

Old Spanish Well and Chimney 1671–1695

Location

East of State Road A1A behind the Anastasia Baptist Church. Immediately south of Anastasia Baptist Church, turn onto San Juan Street and proceed eastward one block to Old Beach Road; turn right on Old Beach Road and go one block south. The well and chimney are located at the intersection of Old Beach Road and Riviera Street.

Visitor information

A state historical marker is posted at the site. The Old Spanish Well and Chimney are situated on county-owned land. Parking is available on a small lot beside the site.

History

The Old Spanish Well and Chimney are all that remain of what may have been a Spanish barracks complex that housed the quarry overseer, master masons, and stonecutters employed to mine coquina for construction of the Castillo de San Marcos. The Spanish began building the great military fortress in 1672, which serves to date this site, for not until then did the Spanish colonists begin to carve coquina out of the ground in quantity. The most distinctive building material used in St. Augustine, coquina is found in extensive deposits along Florida's northeast coast. Anastasia Island contains the most significant deposits of the stone in St. Johns County. Under the supervision of overseer Alonso Díaz Mejía, the coquina quarries on Anastasia Island were opened in 1671 specifically to provide stone for construction of the Castillo. Great blocks of it were carved

from the pits, placed on wagons, and hauled some three miles westward across the Matanzas River to the Castillo construction site. Leftover stones from that enormous project were subsequently used for many other buildings in the city, giving St. Augustine a distinctive appearance. The walls of most of the thirty-six surviving colonial structures in the city were fashioned from coquina.

Old Spanish Quarries 1600s

Location

The colonial quarries are located within Anastasia State Recreation Area on Anastasia Island. Enter through the main gateway to the park on Anastasia State Park Road, on the east side of State Road A1A, across that highway from the St. Augustine Alligator Farm and Zoological Park, about one mile south of the Bridge of Lions.

Visitor information

A descriptive green and gold state historical marker is posted at the entrance to the quarry site, immediately upon entering the Anastasia State Recreation Area. A short walk beneath a canopy of trees brings the visitor to the quarries. The pits created by the mining of the coquina are still visible. The state park service has posted a number of informational signs along the wooded walkway to the site.

History

Coquina is a quarried stone, formed over the ages from donax shells fused in large deposits by calcium carbonate. The deposits of the rare stone, which lie close to the surface, are found in greatest quantity along the northeastern coast of Florida. The Spanish discovered the material not long after their arrival in 1565, though they continued for another century to build their houses from wood. Enough of the

stone was carved from the ground to build a powder house in 1598, undoubtedly the city's first masonry structure. In the late seventeenth century, the Spanish began to excavate the stone in massive quantities to construct the Castillo de San Marcos. The soft stone absorbed enemy cannon shot without splintering into grenadelike fragments. The most significant deposits of the material in St. Johns County are found on Anastasia Island, where sixteen coquina quarries, called the Old Spanish Quarries, were opened. The stones carved from these quarries were used to build the fortress and, in the early eighteenth century, many residential buildings throughout the colonial city. Most of the thirty-six surviving colonial structures in St. Augustine contain walls built with stones dug from these quarries.

Anastasia State Recreation Area 1565 to the present

Location

Along the Atlantic Coast, on the northern tip of Anastasia Island. The main entrance is located on the east side of State Road A1A, across that highway from the St. Augustine Alligator Farm and Zoological Park, about one mile south of the Bridge of Lions.

Visitor information

Anastasia State Recreation Area, owned and maintained by the state of Florida, is publicly accessible seven days a week during normal business hours. The narrow spit of barrier island containing the park is compressed between the Atlantic Ocean and Salt Run, a tidal lagoon. Driving on the four miles of white, sandy beach within the park is prohibited, though parking is available at its southern entrance. The park contains 139 campsites.

History

The northern tip of Anastasia Island, including the state park, has been closely associated with the defense and maritime history of St. Augustine since the sixteenth century. The historic sea entrance to St. Augustine once ran through what is now known as Salt Run,

at the north end of Anastasia State Recreation Area. Pedro Menéndez de Avilés, the founder of St. Augustine, sailed through the inlet in 1565 on his voyage of settlement. The U.S. Army Corps of Engineers closed the channel in 1947 and carved a new inlet farther to the north. The park also contains veins of coquina, the distinctive stone quarried for the walls of the Castillo de San Marcos and many other structures in the city. Ocean bathing on the beaches of this area became a favorite diversion for winter tourists during the Flagler Era (1886–1913), leading to the construction of a pavilion, attractions (such as the original St. Augustine Alligator Farm, which was located just south of the present park site), and a tram railway that carried passengers from St. Augustine to what is now St. Augustine Beach. Anastasia State Recreation Area remains one of Florida's most popular recreational destinations.

Fish Island Site 1763–1821

Location
The east side of the Matanzas River, north of the approach to State Road 312

Visitor information
Fish Island, all of it privately owned, is accessible by public road. It is best seen from the eastern side of the Mickler-O'Connell Bridge over State Road 312. Remnants of the island plantation's archaeological ruins have been preserved.

History
Fish Island is named for Jesse Fish, a British subject who resided in St. Augustine from 1736 until his death in 1790. As a young boy in St. Augustine, Fish learned the Spanish language and local customs and rose to become the St. Augustine representative of the Walton Company, a British firm that supplied the Spanish garrison with provisions. His tenure as a businessman spanned six decades, three periods of the city's colonial history, and two transfers of power. In 1764, when the Spanish evacuated the colony, and in 1784, when the British were

forced to leave, Fish acted as the agent for many property owners who had to abandon their lands. Jesse Fish developed his own plantation on Fish Island. He named it *El Vergel,* or The Garden. The forty-acre orchard he planted there became internationally famous for the oranges it produced. One of the first successful commercial orange groves in Florida, El Vergel also produced figs, peaches, pomegranates, and limes. Almost from the time of his death in 1790, speculative mystery has surrounded Fish's activities in St. Augustine as one of the very few, if not only, persons of European origin to continue living in the area through two transfers of international ownership.

Summer Haven Late 1800s

Location
Summer Haven is located on the east side of A1A, on the south side of Matanzas Inlet, approximately sixteen miles south of St. Augustine.

Visitor information
Summer Haven is accessible by public road. The historic residences are privately owned, but most can be viewed from the public right-of-way.

History
Summer Haven numbers itself among the oldest beach communities on the east coast of Florida, a seasonal resort from the time of its late-nineteenth-century origins.

The Lodge

Linked to St. Augustine by the Matanzas River (Intracoastal Waterway), Summer Haven began as a sleepy retreat, populated by Northerners during winter months and some St. Johns County residents during summers. Among the more prominent winter residents were the Mellons from Pittsburgh, Pennsylvania, whose fortune was derived from steel and finance. Thomas Mellon, one of the heirs to the Mellon family fortune, found the location refreshing and built a small vacation retreat here in 1882. His cottage survived a hurricane that same year. In 1895 Mellon built a large house next door, called The Lodge, a five-bedroom Cracker-style building, identified by its pyramidal roof and wrap-around veranda, as pictured above. The Lodge was carefully restored in 2002. Summer Haven, with a waterfront location that offered access to both the ocean and the river, remained a popular destination for winter residents and tourists through the 1920s. Until that time, the only access to the location was by water along the Intracoastal Waterway. Summer Haven's rustic, seaside cottages portray a period of tourist-related history in Florida that is fast disappearing amid the high-rise condominiums that increasingly clutter the state's coastline.

Location

The oceanfront along A1A north of State Road 206, in the vicinity of Crescent Beach

Visitor information

Butler Beach and Frank Butler Park are both open to the public daily.

History

Butler Beach is named for Frank B. Butler (1885–1973), the leading black businessman in St. Johns County during the early twentieth century. In 1914, Butler began selling meats and groceries from the Palace Market at 87-1/2 Washington Street in Lincolnville, a St. Augustine neighborhood settled in the nineteenth century by the descendants of slaves. A fine businessman, Butler expanded his interests to include real estate and he organized the College Park Realty Company in time to reap advantage from the great land boom of the 1920s. In 1927, he acquired a stretch of undeveloped oceanfront property about ten miles south of St. Augustine in order to provide a public beach for African-Americans. Excluded from facilities frequented by whites, they were denied access to the county's beaches at a time in the early twentieth century when beach-going had become a popular form of recreation for Americans. Butler's Beach became quickly popular, attracting African-Americans from throughout northeast Florida. Some eleven businesses within the site catered to sunbathers in the late 1940s. Butler continued to expand his holdings along the beach, continuing to purchase additional property as late as 1949. In 1958, by purchase and a gift from Frank Butler, the state of Florida gained title to the property, which it converted to a park named in honor of the man who served so well the people of his community. The park is managed by St. Johns County.

Fort Matanzas National Monument (1742)

Location
Fourteen miles south of St. Augustine on State Road A1A, north of the Matanzas Inlet

Visitor information
Fort Matanzas is a federally owned property managed by the U. S. National Park Service and accessible to the public daily as a historical attraction. Park Service rangers provide guided tours of the monument. Visitors must cross the Intracoastal Waterway by ferry.

History
Built in the aftermath of the British invasion of 1740, Fort Matanzas demonstrates the determination of Spanish colonial authorities to defend St. Augustine against a renewed attack from the sea. Completed in 1742, the fortification, erected on the west bank of the Matanzas River, enabled Spanish gunners to monitor enemy ships entering the inlet south of it in order to attack St. Augustine from the water. Cannons mounted on the gundeck of the fort could easily menace any ship proceeding along the waterway. The fort takes its name from its proximity to the site where some three hundred Frenchmen were captured and put to the sword by the troops of Pedro Menéndez de Avilés in 1565, shortly after the landing of his colonizing expedition. The first structure at this site, a watchtower, was constructed in the late sixteenth century. Fort

VCB

Matanzas fell into disrepair in the century after Spain ceded Florida to the United States. It was restored in the 1930s. Fort Matanzas and the Castillo de San Marcos, its companion site in St. Augustine proper, are the only two remaining Spanish military fortifications within the continental United States.

Massacre of the French, Matanzas Inlet

Location

State Highway A1A, just south of the Mantanzas Inlet Bridge

Visitor information

A green historic marker stands along a public right-of-way, south of Fort Mantazas National Monument. Visitors may park along the right-of-way in order to read the marker text.

History

In 1564 the French planted a settlement they named Fort Caroline near the mouth of the St. Johns River—some forty miles north of present-day St. Augustine—from which they intended to solidify their command of the Florida peninsula. The Spanish, who claimed Florida as their own, viewed the Protestant French Huguenots as heretical intruders upon Spanish territory, though the Spanish had earlier abandoned their own attempts to settle the peninsula. In 1565, however, the king of Spain, Philip II, appointed Pedro Menéndez de Avilés—one of the ablest Spanish naval officers of his day—to lead a colonizing expedition to Florida. Philip desired to prevent Spain's enemies from establishing a military position on the northeast coast of Florida from which they might menace the Spanish treasure fleets, loaded with precious cargo of silver and gold that sailed the Gulf current along Florida's east coast. Learning of the French presence, Philip ordered Menéndez to extinguish the colony. In the fall of 1565, Menéndez, at the head of a large band of soldiers and colonists, landed on the Florida coast and established the settlement at St. Augustine. The French at once set sail from Fort Caroline to attack the Spanish settlement, but a severe storm drove them ashore. The Spanish captured some three hundred French survivors of the expedition. They put most to the sword near this inlet, which was thereafter called Matanzas, meaning "slaughter."

Matanzas Inlet Bridge

Area Six
St. Johns County

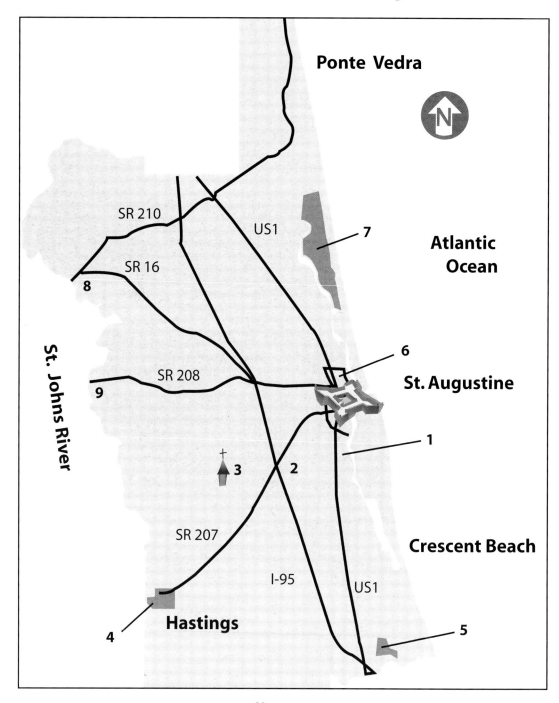

Ponte Vedra

N

SR 210

US1

7

Atlantic
Ocean

SR 16

8

St. Johns River

SR 208

6

St. Augustine

9

1

3

2

SR 207

Crescent Beach

I-95

US1

4

Hastings

5

1 O'Brien-Kelley House 92

2 Treaty Park 93

3 St. Ambrose Catholic Church 94

4 Hastings 95

5 Faver Dykes State Park 96

6 Fort Mose 97

7 Guana River State Park 98

8 William Bartram Trail 99

9 Picolata 100

O'Brien-Kelley House 1885

Location
In the vicinity of St. Augustine Shores, along the west bank of the Matanzas River near Vaill Point

Visitor information
The O'Brien-Kelley House, situated on private property, is not accessible to the public. A boat trip on the Matanzas River southward from St. Augustine affords the best view of the house.

History
The O'Brien-Kelley House, which overlooks the Matanzas River from a sloping bank south of St. Augustine, may be the most architecturally impressive historic residence in rural St. Johns County. The building displays the Queen Anne style of architecture with its irregular form, conical tower, belvedere, encircling veranda, and massive chimneys. Of further significance is the fact that its walls consist of poured concrete, a construction method introduced to America in St. Augustine around the time this house was built. The O'Brien-Kelley House thus joins the Villa Zorayda, the Flagler Era churches in St. Augustine, and the Cordova, Alcazar, and Ponce de Leon hotels as the earliest poured concrete buildings in the United States. The Queen Anne style gained popularity in America upon its introduction at the 1876 Centennial celebration in Philadelphia and remained a favored high-style residential design through the turn of the century. The house was originally constructed in 1885 for Henry Stanton O'Brien of Albany, New York, as a winter home. In 1931, though, it became the Dixie Home for the Aged and Infirm Deaf. During the early 1940s, it was purchased by the Kelleys of Lawrenceville, Georgia, who retained ownership of the property for more than four decades. Under new ownership in the late 1990s, the house was rehabilitated.

photo by Kenneth Barrett

Treaty Park

Location

A historic marker stands along the west side of Wildwood Drive, which connects with State Road 207 about one mile east of U.S. Interstate 95. Treaty Park is approximately one mile south of the intersection of Wildwood Drive and State Road 207.

Visitor information

Two historic markers have been placed at Treaty Park. An earlier one was relocated from the approximate site of the treaty signing at Moultrie Creek. No direct association exists between either marker and the actual site of the treaty signing. The markers are located at the center of the park.

History

The Treaty of Moultrie Creek culminated seventeen days of negotiations between the United States government and the most diverse representative group of Seminoles ever assembled in Florida. The Seminoles were comparative newcomers to Florida, refugees driven, in the 1700s, from the English colonies north of the peninsula. They took up lands once occupied by native Florida tribes, which by the mid-1700s had been all but wiped out by disease and warfare. American settlers after 1821 sought removal of the Indians from north Florida in an attempt to grab the tribal lands. Approximately 425 Seminoles attended the meeting at Moultrie Creek. They were led by thirty-two chiefs, who signed the negotiated document. The treaty, ratified by the U.S. Senate on December 23, 1823, established a four-million-acre reservation for the Indians in the central part of the peninsula. The treaty failed, however, to eliminate tensions between white settlers and the tribe. Clashes between the two groups continued and ultimately led to the outbreak in 1835 of the largest and longest Indian conflict in the history of the United States, the Second Seminole War. The seven-year-long war resulted in the destruction of virtually every white settlement along the east coast of Florida south of St. Augustine.

St. Ambrose Catholic Church 1907

Location
Moccasin Branch, north of State Road 207. From Elkton, which straddles State Road 207 west of St. Augustine, travel west 2.8 miles on St. Ambrose Church Road to Church Road. Turn left on Church Road and proceed one-half mile to the church property.

Visitor information
This is an active church. Interior access is generally permitted only during worship hours on Saturdays and Sundays.

History

Since the late eighteenth century, the Minorcans have formed a distinct and important part of the population of St. Augustine and St. Johns County. Although referred to generically as "Minorcans," the immigrants and their descendants to whom the name historically has been attached actually consisted of Greeks, Spaniards, and Italians, as well as residents of the island of Minorca. They arrived in St. Johns County as refugees from a failed colony established at what is today the city of New Smyrna Beach. Some of the New Smyrna Colony refugees settled at Moccasin Branch, a rural area west of St. Augustine, and became the core parishioners of the St. Ambrose Parish, organized by Father Stephen Langlade in 1875. In 1878, the parishioners acquired land for a cemetery and a parish hall. Father Langlade arranged for the Sisters of St. Joseph to open a school at the St. Ambrose Church in 1881. Classroom instruction continued there until 1948. The present parish church, constructed in 1907, and the surrounding buildings, resting beneath moss-draped live oak trees, offer a picturesque view of a rural Catholic community.

Hastings

Location

On State Road 207, approximately eighteen miles west of St. Augustine. Downtown Hastings is located along Main Street, north of State Road 207.

Visitor information

A historic marker stands next to the Hastings City Hall. Parking is easily available.

History

The late-nineteenth-century arrival of the railroad in St. Augustine and the subsequent growth of a thriving tourist industry spurred the organization of new communities and the expansion of existing ones in the

essentially rural countryside that surrounded the Ancient City. Principal among the towns that developed on the periphery of St. Augustine was Hastings, established in 1890 by Thomas Hastings, a cousin of Henry Flagler. The town of Hastings, located in the western part of the county, was promoted as the center of an experimental farm designed to provide a source of fresh produce for Flagler's hotels. His railroad company ran a spur to the town and constructed a station there. The rail line served the town and its surrounding farms well in following decades by carrying their produce to more distant markets when Flagler's hotels began to close. Soil conditions in southwestern St. Johns County especially favored potato growing. Reflecting the importance of the potato industry and the cooperative marketing movement, the Potato Growers Building, pictured here, was completed in 1927. The stately building, decorated with quoins at the four corners of two square towers that straddle a recessed entrance, housed the local farmer-owned and -controlled potato marketing organization.

In 1918, a scarcity of potatoes in northern markets boosted the price of potatoes, the main cash crop for Hastings farmers, to an astronomical $20 a barrel. Buyers from throughout the east coast rushed in, their pockets filled with ready cash. So much money flowed into the local bank that town officials called upon the state militia to protect the building. Uniformed men patrolled the streets of Hastings each night, awaiting the next day's arrival of armored trucks to haul the cash to Jacksonville for safekeeping.

Faver Dykes State Park 1815 to the present

Location

Accessible from U.S. 1 South, north of its intersection with U.S. Interstate 95, seventeen miles south of St. Augustine. Pellicer Creek forms the north boundary of the park.

Visitor information

The state of Florida owns and maintains Faver Dykes State Park. The park is open to the public daily from 8:00 A.M. to sunset. The park offers a boat ramp, fishing dock, canoe and camp rentals, campsites, a picnic area, and nature trails.

History

Faver Dykes State Park is situated on a wooded tract that was part of a large land grant conceded by the Spanish government in 1815 to Joseph Hernandez, a St. Augustine resident of Minorcan descent. Sugar planter, attorney, Florida's first territorial delegate to the U.S. Congress, and brigadier general in the Florida militia during the Second Seminole War (1835–1842), Hernandez played a major role in the economic and political life of St. Augustine and East Florida during the early nineteenth century. On Pellicer Creek, named for another Minorcan, Francisco Pellicer, Hernandez owned a plantation known in Spanish as *Buena Suerte,* or Good Luck. Hernandez's property eventually came into the possession of the Faver family.

Hiram Faver, longtime clerk of the Circuit Court of St. Johns County, donated seven hundred acres of the land to the Florida State Board of Parks in December 1950. The park created at the site was named for his parents, Alexander H. Faver and Ellen Dykes Faver.

Fort Mose 1738–1740 and 1752–1763

Location

An undeveloped area in the north end of St. Augustine, close to the west bank of the Intracoastal Waterway (North River), approximately one mile north of the Castillo de San Marcos. The Fort Mose site is accessible from U.S. 1 at the north city limits.

Visitor information

Though the remains of the two forts are no longer visible, a wooden walkway permits access to a part of the coastal lagoon within which the two were originally erected. Construction of a visitor center was completed in 2007. There is ample parking next to the visitor center.

History

Escaped African-born slaves fleeing British plantations in the Carolinas and seeking refuge and freedom in the Spanish colony of Florida often made their way south to St. Augustine in the late 1600s and early 1700s. Spanish officials gave the escaped slaves permission to establish their own community, Gracia Real de Santa Teresa de Mosé, the first legally sanctioned free black community in what is now the United States. The men in the town of free blacks were enlisted into the Spanish militia. They served as the first line of defense against British attack from the north. The militia who manned the first site of Fort Mose took part in a number of major battles, beginning in 1740 when the British governor of Georgia, James Oglethorpe, led an invading army of British troops in an attack against St. Augustine and Spanish Florida. Rebuilt at a new site after that conflict, the second Fort Mose was abandoned in 1763, when Spain ceded Florida to Great Britain; its inhabitants moved to Cuba. In the 1980s, the state of Florida acquired the grounds containing the historic site, which it made a part of its park system. State officials, assisted by the Fort Mose Historical Society, plan to reconstruct on the site a version of the first free black community in America.

Guana River State Park
seventeenth to twentieth centuries

Location

Guana River State Park is an 11,500-acre tract nestled between the Intracoastal Waterway and Florida Highway Road A1A along St. Johns County's northern beach. Its southern boundary lies about four miles north of the Frank and Mary Usina Bridge, close to the main highway entrance to the Environmental Education Center.

Visitor information

The state of Florida owns and maintains Guana River State Park, which it acquired in 1983. Accessible during daylight hours, the park offers a rare view of the natural environment along the state's northeastern coastline. There are a number of entrances to the park off Florida Highway A1A. Recreational opportunities abound, including fishing, boating, and beach access. There is a small entrance fee to the park. The Environmental Education Center offers exceptional exhibits.

History

Historic sites within the park date to the seventeenth century and include a colonial Spanish mission, the Nativity of Our Lady of Tolomato, located in the tract at what is now Wright's Landing. During the British Period (1763–1784), a number of British loyalists who were forced out of colonies to the north took brief refuge within the boundaries of the park along the Tolomato River. Subsequently, during the Second Spanish Period (1784–1821), the area became the setting for thirty-seven Spanish land grants, issued by the Spanish government in the waning years of its control over Florida. Scattered settlements continued to appear during the nineteenth and twentieth centuries. Known sites within the park include dike networks, levees and ditches, a sawmill, individual homesteads, and a historic cemetery. *Guano,* Spanish for moss or palm thatch, appeared as "Guana" on a map drawn by British Surveyor William Gerard DeBrahm in 1769 and subsequently became the name commonly applied to the area by English-speaking settlers.

William Bartram Trail 1765–1766 and 1771–1773

Location
The part of the trail that runs through St. Johns County is found between State Road 207 and Julington Creek along State Road 13.

Visitor information
The Bartram Trail generally follows State Road 13, in a picturesque rural area of St. Johns County that is rapidly disappearing. Various historic places, including Tocoi, Picolata, and Switzerland, are also located on the route of the Bartram Trail. Markers describing the trail are found at Picolata and Switzerland.

History
John Bartram of Philadelphia, regarded in the eighteenth century as the greatest botanist in the New World, founded the first botanical garden in America in 1728. He was later appointed Royal Botanist to King George III. In 1765, some ten years before the start of the American Revolutionary War and shortly after the British acquired Florida from Spain, John and his son William made a celebrated journey through present-day North Carolina, South Carolina, Georgia, Alabama, Tennessee, Mississippi, Louisiana, and Florida. John later published a journal of their travels. William, the first native-born American naturalist to achieve international acclaim, returned to Florida nearly a decade later and wrote a travel account that gained the attention of the European literary world. Their writings provided the first accurate descriptions of the flora and fauna in Florida at a time when curiosity about the peninsula began to appear in the literary salons of Europe. The Bartram Trail traces the route they took through St. Johns County. Virtually unchecked and headlong modern development threatens to destroy the natural beauty the Bartrams encountered here.

Location

A historic marker stands at the junction of State Road 13 and State Road 208, where the historic route of the Picolata Road from the St. Johns River to St. Augustine began.

Visitor information

The historic marker rests in the approximate middle of Picolata, the name historically attached to this amorphous, picturesque, rural part of western St. Johns County. Historians believe they have found the location of the Spanish fort. No trace of it remains above ground. They also identified, in 1996, the remains of the Civil War fort, about a half-mile south of the site of the earlier Spanish fort. At the time of this writing, the highly visible remnants of the artillery earthworks that once defended the Civil War fort, one of the very few such sites in Florida, remain largely ignored and forgotten.

History

Picolata remained a significant transportation and military site from its establishment during the First Spanish Period (1565–1763) through the Civil War (1861–1865). Located at a strategic crossing of the St. Johns River, Picolata provided access to the Apalachee Indian missions to the west, to points north and south along the river, and eastward to St. Augustine. In 1734, Spanish Governor Francisco del Moral Sánchez ordered construction of a blockhouse, barracks, storehouses, and batteries at Picolata. In 1740 British troops under the command of General James Oglethorpe of Georgia drove Spanish defenders from the riverside fort. In 1765 the British signed a treaty at Picolata with Florida Indians that defined the limits of Indian settlement throughout the peninsula. General Winfield Scott established his headquarters here for a time in early 1836 to plan his campaign for the Second Seminole War (1835–1842). Among the troops stationed there during that conflict was a young lieutenant, William Tecumseh Sherman. The Union Army maintained a large garrison at Picolata for much of the Civil War. The Picolata Road remained the major land route from the river to St. Augustine until the arrival of the railroad in the late nineteenth century.

Picolata, along the St. Johns River

Unmarked St. Johns County Sites

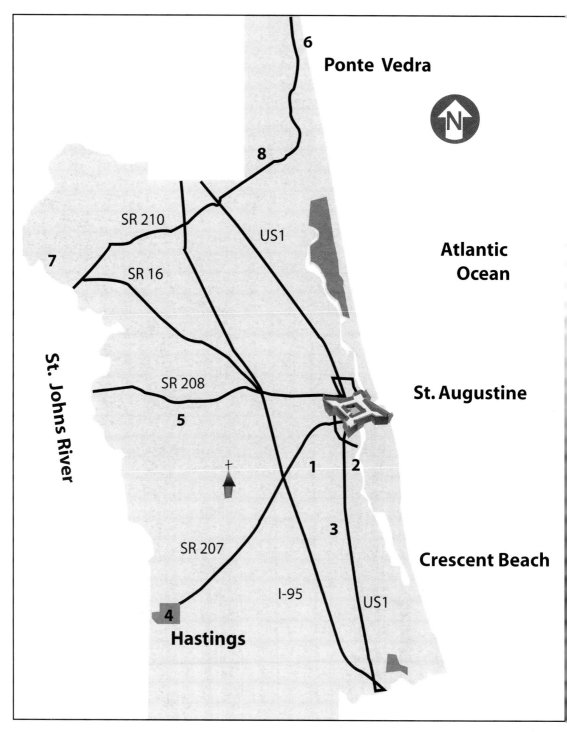

1 Osceola Capture Site   104
2 Moultrie   104
3 Old Kings Road   105
4 Dixie Highway   105
5 Theatrical Troupe Massacre Site 106
6 Operation Pastorius   106
7 Switzerland   107
8 Fort San Diego, or Diego Plains   107

Osceola Capture Site (October, 1837)

A marker buried in the ground and all but impossible to find in the south-central part of St. Johns County once marked the site of an event that captured the nation's attention during the Second Seminole War (1835–1842). The war resulted from decades of conflict between settlers and Seminoles. In 1823 the Treaty of Moultrie Creek established a four-million-acre reservation for the Indians, but failed to eliminate the tensions that had developed between the two parties. Open hostilities erupted in late 1835. After nearly two years of fighting, the Seminoles, under their leader, Osceola, agreed in October 1837 to meet with U.S. Army officials in a clearing near St. Augustine to discuss a settlement of the conflict. Gen. Joseph Hernandez, commander of the East Florida Militia, acting under orders, seized the famous Seminole Indian and seventy of his braves, who had assembled at this site under a flag of truce. The Seminoles were taken to St. Augustine and imprisoned at Fort Marion (Castillo de San Marcos). Osceola's fellow chieftain, Coacoochee, and nineteen other Indians among the more than one hundred men, women, and children held in the Castillo, managed a daring escape from the fortress prison barely a month later. Osceola, in poor health from malaria, remained incarcerated and was later removed to Fort Moultrie, South Carolina, where he died in captivity. Many Americans at the time regarded the seizure of Osceola under a flag of truce as an act of treachery. Gen. Thomas S. Jesup, who ordered the capture, found himself even twenty years later responding to criticism. As for Osceola, the event secured his image as a romantic, betrayed warrior.

Moultrie (1763–1784)

British rule in 1763 brought with it to Florida the plantation system and its dependence on slave labor. A number of plantations along the St. Johns River and what is now the Intracoastal Waterway produced, principally, indigo, naval stores, and rice. Two of the largest planters in British East Florida, John Imrie and John Moultrie, carved their plantations out of the wooded lands surrounding what became known as Moultrie Creek. Both were primarily devoted to the production of naval stores, mainly tars and turpentine extracted from the resin of pine trees. The substances found a variety of uses in colonial times, particularly in the shipbuilding industry. John Moultrie, who also served as a lieutenant governor of East Florida during the British Period, the time of the American Revolution, gave his name to both the locale—located about three miles south of St. Augustine along U.S. 1— and to the broad creek that flows quietly between picturesque bluffs, an unusual topographic feature in St. Johns County.

Old Kings Road (1771–1775)

Originally constructed during the British Period (1763–1784), the Old Kings Road ran from Mosquitos (now New Smyrna Beach) to the colonies of Georgia and South Carolina. Begun in earnest in 1771 and essentially completed by 1775, the road provided the principal avenue of transportation in British East Florida, a role it continued to fulfill during the following half-century. It linked Savannah and Charleston to the settlements and plantations lining Florida's east coast, which stretched from New Smyrna to St. Augustine. The road was completed just in time to accommodate the flight south to Florida of British loyalists driven from their homes in the Carolinas and Georgia during the Revolutionary War. After the evacuation of New Smyrna in 1777 and the return of the Spanish in 1784, the road was comparatively neglected, though for the next 150 years and more parts of it were converted into new roads and highways. Modern development has obscured much of the Old Kings Road. In a few places scattered throughout St. Johns, Flagler, and Volusia Counties, its traces can still be discerned as a faint opening in thick vegetation. In other places, the old road has been converted into modern streets or highways. One such section in southern St. Johns County continues to bear the name "Old Kings Road."

Dixie Highway (1917)

Completed in 1917, the Dixie Highway, a brick road running from St. Augustine to Hastings and some points south, provided a vital link in the development of a highway system within St. Johns County. The road eventually made its way along the east coast of Florida to Miami, becoming one of the state's first major tourist thoroughfares. The Dixie Highway encouraged expansion of commercial agriculture around communities such as Hastings, Spuds, and Elkton in the southwestern part of the county. But most importantly, the highway appeared at a time when Americans were beginning their love affair with the automobile. In barely a decade's time, the mechanical evolution of the technologically primitive "horseless carriage" to a fast-moving, sturdy vehicle capable of spanning vast distances created major changes in American society. The automobile not only altered the map of Florida, but led to a wholesale change in the state's economy. Tourism, an industry previously dominated by relatively wealthy travelers who arrived by railroad, began to feed upon a far more numerous class of middle-income visitors who used the newly built highways to find their way to the "land of vacations and sunshine." A small section of the original brick road can still be found about three miles south of Hastings at the intersection of Hastings Boulevard and Cracker Swamp Road.

Theatrical Troupe Massacre Site (May 23, 1840)

The Second Seminole War (1835–1842) grew out of years of conflict between the United States and the Seminole Indian Tribe. The Treaty of Moultrie Creek, negotiated in 1823, established a four-million-acre reservation for the Indians, but it failed to eliminate tensions between the tribe and the white settlers. Frequent clashes between Indians and settlers led to an outbreak of hostilities in 1835. During the war, St. Johns County was the setting for limited action between the combatants and was generally thought at the time to offer safe harbor to many white settlers from outlying parts of the eastern peninsula. On Saturday, May 23, 1840, a theatrical troupe and other travelers making their way to St. Augustine by stage coach from the river landing at Picolata were attacked by Coacoochee (Wild Cat) and a band of marauding Seminoles. The Indians killed one member the troupe and four other passengers. The surviving thespians proceeded to St. Augustine where, despite their misfortune, they conducted performances for the next two weeks. Several Indians were spotted some months later garbed in Shakespearian costumes plundered from the baggage wagon. A state historic marker beside State Road 208 (Picolata Road), about one mile west of I-95 in rural St. Johns County, stands near the site of the "massacre."

Operation Pastorius (June 16, 1942)

In the early months of World War II, eight German saboteurs came ashore in the dark of night on the east coast, agents in the only major espionage mission conducted in the continental United States during that war. The first team of four landed on a deserted beach in Long Island, New York. Then, just before dawn on June 16, 1942, German submarine U-584 surfaced off the coast at Ponte Vedra to discharge four more agents on the northern shoreline of St. Johns County. Operating under the code name "Operation Pastorius," they were given a broad range of destructive tasks designed to cripple U.S. industry. Once on land, the saboteurs walked seven miles north to Jacksonville Beach, where they caught a bus to downtown Jacksonville and registered at the Mayflower and Seminole Hotels. The mission proved a spectacular failure. Before the month's end, two members of the Long Island team betrayed the operation and, within days, the FBI rounded up all eight. None had even attempted an act of sabotage. At the direction of President Franklin D. Roosevelt, a military tribunal was convened in the nation's capital to judge the fate of the Nazi saboteurs. The two informants received jail sentences and in 1948 were set free and returned to Germany. The remaining six were executed by electric chair on August 8, 1942. A historic marker describing this event stands in front of the Ponte Vedra Inn and Club, four miles north of the saboteurs' actual landing site, which occurred near the 900 block of Ponte Vedra Boulevard.

Switzerland (1763–1821)

Now engulfed by unchecked modern residential development and marred by commercial strip malls, Switzerland, the site of a Revolutionary War–era plantation in northwest St. Johns County, is noted only by a historic marker standing on the east side of State Road 13 near the Switzerland Community Church, about five miles south of Julington Creek. Francis P. Fatio, a Swiss immigrant, received a ten-thousand-acre grant from the British government in the 1770s to settle this swath of land along the St. Johns River. Known as New Switzerland, the Fatio plantation became one of the most important producers of naval stores in the region. Fatio became a Spanish subject when the British departed in 1784, and he remained an important figure in East Florida during the Second Spanish Period (1784–1821). The Patriot Rebellion of 1812, an uprising in East Florida against Spanish authority, resulted in the destruction of the plantation buildings, but the place name remained the same.

Fort San Diego, or Diego Plains (ca. 1735–1743)

Located about twenty miles north of St. Augustine, near the headwaters of the North (Tolomato) River, Fort San Diego guarded the major interior water route north of St. Augustine and the haulover (land connection) between Pablo Creek and the St. Johns River. Fort San Diego was originally part of a large cattle ranch owned by a Spanish subject named Diego Espinosa. During the mid-1730s, concerned about the threat of a British invasion from Georgia, Spanish military officials fortified Espinosa's house by constructing a fifteen-foot-high palisade and two bastions. In 1740 the British arrived. Under the command of Georgia Governor James Oglethorpe, they drove off fifty-seven Spanish defenders and made Fort San Diego the field headquarters for a subsequent attack on St. Augustine. Oglethorpe added a ditch and breastwork and used the fort to protect his northern supply lines. Upon his departure from Florida, he destroyed the fortifications, but the Spanish quickly returned and rebuilt them. In 1743 approximately two hundred Indians and a number of English militiamen returned again, destroying the fort and killing forty Spanish defenders. The remains of Fort San Diego were still evident as late as 1858, when they were described by Florida historian George R. Fairbanks. A state historic marker that once stood beside the Palm Valley Road two miles west of Florida Highway A1A to note the site has disappeared.

Index

(Photographs indicated with **bold** text)

Abbott, Lucy, 70
Abbott Tract Historic District, 70, **70**, 72
African-American(s), 32, 49, 50, 51, 86
Alcazar Hotel, 7, **53**, 54, **54**, 55, 56
alligators, 79
Altrusa Club, 42
Alvarez, Gerónimo, 38, 39
America's Gilded Age, 57
American Revolution, 11, 22, 24, 26, 38, 40, 45, 99, 104
Ammidown, Henry Philip, 48
Anastasia Baptist Church, 81
Anastasia Island, 14, 16, 33, 48, 76–89, 80, 81, 82, 83
Anastasia State Recreation Area, 82, 83, **83**
Ancient City, 22, 37, 46, 49, 61, 78, 95
Ancient City Baptist Church, 53, 65, **65**, 66
Anderson, Dr. Andrew, 60
Anderson, Dr. Andrew, Jr., 60
Apalache, 19,
Apalachee Indians, 100
Avero House (St. Photios Shrine), 22, **22**, 24

Bacchus Club, 74
Bartram, John, 99
Bartram, William, 99
Bartram Trail (see William Bartram Trail)
Baskin, Norton, 71
Bicentennial, 28
Bonaparte, Napoleon, 11, 46
Boom Period, 64, 70
Bridge of Lions, 28, 33, **33**, 60, 78, 79, 80, 82, 83
British East Florida, 11, 26, 40, 104, 105, 107
British West Florida, 11
Bronson Cottage, 45, **45**
Buena Suerte (plantation), 96
Butler, Frank B., 49, 86
Butler Beach and Frank Butler Park, 49, 86, **86**

Camino Real, 19
campanile (bell tower), 30
cannon(s), 80, 87
    balls, 39, 78
    shot, 78, 82
Canova, Antonio, 47
Canova, Judy, 47
Canova, John, 47
Canova House, 47, **47**
Carcaba, P. F., 61
Carcaba, W.H., 61
Carlos, King Juan, 27
Carnegie Institute, 17, 42
Carrere, John M., 57, 62, 66
Carrere and Hastings, 54
"Casa del Canonaza," 39
Casa Monica Hotel, 53, 56, **56**
Castillo de San Marcos National Monument, 9, 14, **14**, 15, 16, 17, 18, 19, 31, 33, 38, 70, 71, 74, 78, 81, 82, 83, 87, 97, 104
Cathedral Basilica of St. Augustine, **10**, 30, **30**
cemeteries, 20, **20**, 41, **41**, 42, 67, **67**, 72, 94, 98
Chinese Chippendale, 44
churches, 7, 22, 30, **30**, 32, **32**, 43, 49, 50, **50**, 51, **51**, 58, 62, **62**, 63, 64, 65, **65**, 66, **66**, 72, 81, 92, 94, **94**, 107
cigar-making, 61
City Gate, **8**, 17, 18, 19, **19**, 20, 21
City Hall, 7, 53, 54
City of St. Augustine, 15, 18, 19, 26, 54, 60, 78
Civil War, 11, 19, 24, 28, 36, 39, 44, 45, 49, 51, 60, 67, 70, 100
Coacoochee (wild cat), 104, 106
Col. Upham Cottage, 44, **44**
College Park Realty Company, 86
Colonial City Historic District, 16, **16**, 38, 43
Colonial Dames, 37
colonial era, 28, 51
    building(s) of the, 17, 21, 22, 40

historic resources of the, 16
    Spanish builders of the, 23
    Spanish, 51
    wells from the, 28
colonial Florida, 48
Colonial Revival style, 45, 63
Colonial Town Plaza, 28, **28**, 29
colonies
    English, 11, 14, 93, 98
    of Georgia and South Carolina, 105
    Spanish, 28
colony,
    British, at New Smyrna, 21, 22, 47, 94
    former, 20
    of Georgia, 78
    Spanish, of Florida, 11, 39, 40, 42, 72, 84, 88, 97
Confederate
    general, 36
    officer, 36
Confederate War Memorial, 28
Constitution Monument, 28, 29, **29**
coquina, 14, 15, 19, 23, 24, 32, 36, 41, 42, 46, 78, 81, 82, 83
Cracker style, 85
crocodile, 79
Cubo Line of Defense, 18, **18**, 19

Dade, Major Francis L., 41
Davis, Alexander Jackson, 45
Daytona Museum of Arts and Sciences, 46
de Mesa Sánchez House, 23, **23**, 24
de Montiano, Governor Manuel, 78
DeBrahm, William Gerard, 98
dei Lanzi, Loggia, 33
del Moral Sánchez, Governor Francisco, 100
Depression Era, 15
Diaz Mejía, Alonso, 81
Diocese of St. Augustine, 30, 72
Dixie Highway, 105
Dixie Home for the Aged and Infirm Deaf, 92
donax shells, 82

Drexel, Mother Katherine, 51
Dunham, Judge David R., 37

East Florida (*see* British East
    Florida)
El Vergel (plantation), 84
Elixio de la Puente, J. J., 43
Emerson, Ralph Waldo, 46
Environmental Education Center,
    98
Episcopal, 50
Espinosa, Diego, 107
Everglades, 63
Exchange Bank Building
    (Exchange Bank of St.
    Augustine), 31, **31**

Fairbanks, George R., 107
Fatio, Francis P., 107
Fatio, Louisa, 37
Faver, Alexander H., 96
Faver, Ellen Dykes, 96
Faver, Hiram, 96
Faver Dykes State Park, 96, **96**
Ferdinand VII, King, 29
Fernández, Pedro, 42
Fernández-Llambias House, 42,
    42
First National Bank of St.
    Augustine, 31
Fish, Jesse, 42, 84
Fish Island Site, 84, **84**
Fishwick, William, 59
flag
    illuminated, 41
    of Spain, 11
    of truce, 104
Flagler, Jennie Louise, 62
Flagler, Henry, 11, 54, 56, 57, 58,
    60, 61, 62, 63, 64, 65, 66,
    71, 74, 95
Flagler College, 2, 9, 57, **57**, 60,
    64
Flagler Era, 11, 44, 56, 62, 83, 92
Flagler Memorial Presbyterian
    Church, 53, 62, **62**, 63, 64,
    65, 66
Florida Department of State, 18
Florida Department of
    Transportation, 33
Florida East Coast Railway Co.,
    56, 63, 64
Florida National Guard, 38, 39,

40, 41
Florida State Board of Parks, 96
Florida Territorial Period, 11, 37
Forbes, Reverend John, 32
Fort Marion, 14, 104
Fort Matanzas National
    Monument, **5,** 87, **87**
Fort Mose, 97, **97**
Fort Mose Historical Society, 97
Fort San Diego (Diego Plains),
    107
fortification(s), 14, 73, 87, 107
Fountain of Youth Park, 48, 73,
    73
Franciscan, 40
French Huguenots, 20, 88
French and Indian War, 11

Gannon, Dr. Michael, 48
Garbo, Greta, 46
Garden, The, (plantation) (see *El
    Vergel*)
Genopoly House ("Oldest
    Schoolhouse"), 21, **21**
"gentrification," 49
George III, King, 99
González y Hernández, Tomás, 38
González-Alvarez House ("Oldest
    House"), 38, **38**, 39
Gothic style, 45, 50
Government House, **6,** 27, **27**,
    30
Grace United Methodist Church,
    53, 64, 66, **66**
Gracia Real de Santa Teresa de
    Mosé, 97
Grenadiers, 42
Great Depression, 31, 55
Great Florida Boom, 31
Guana River State Park, 98, **98**

Hardin, General Martin G., 39
Hassett, Father Thomas, 30
Hastings, 95, **95**, **102**, 105
Hastings, Thomas, 57, 62, 66, 95
Havana, 29, 61, 78
Henderich, Fred A., 15, 61
Hernandez, General Joseph, 10,
    96, 104
Historic St. Augustine
    Preservation Board, 7, 17,
    23, 25
Hollingsworth, F. A., 31

Hope, Bob, 47
Hoppin, Howard, 50
hotels, **2, 7,** 9, 54, **54,** 55, 56,
    56, 57, **57,** 58, 60, 61, 62,
    63, 64, 65, 66, 71, 74, 79,
    92, 95, 106
house(s), 6, 21, **21,** 22, **22,** 23,
    23, 24, **24,** 25, **25,** 26, **26,**
    27, **27,** 30, 36, **36,** 37, **37,**
    38, **38,** 39, **39,** 42, **42,** 43,
    43, 44, **44,** 45, **45,** 46, **46,**
    47, **47,** 48, 49, 59, **59,** 63,
    63, 66, 70, 82, 85, **85,** 92,
    92, 107
Huguenots (*see* French
    Huguenots)
hurricane(s), 72, 85
    season, 78

Imrie, John, 104
Ingraham, James E., 63
Ingraham House, 53, 63, **63**
Intracoastal Waterway, 33, 48, 85,
    87, 97, 98, 104

Jesup, General Thomas S., 104

Kellogg, Dr. John Harvey, 59
Kessler, Richard, 56
king of Spain, 24, 88
Kirby Smith, Lt. General
    Edmund, 36
"Kirkside," 64
Komodo dragon, 79

Ladner, John, 44
Langlade, Father Stephen, 94
Lighthouse Park, 80
Lightner, Otto, 54, 55
Lightner Museum, 53, 54, 55, **55**
Lincolnville Historic District, 49,
    49, 50, 51, 86
Lisk, James, 23
Llambias, Catalina Usina, 42
Lodge, The, 85
López de Mendoza Grajales,
    Father Francisco, 72
"Lyndhurst," 45

Margaret's Story, 37
Markland, 53, 60, **60**
Maria Sanchez Creek, 49
Mass, 72

Massacre of the French, Matanzas Inlet, 88, **88**

Matanzas Bay, 16, 33, 48, 70, 72

Matanzas Inlet Bridge, **89**

Matanzas River, 14, 46, 81, 85, 87

Maybeck, Bernard, 57

McKim, Mead and White, 57

McKinnon, K., 59

Mediterranean, 22, 31, 33, 57

Mediterranean Revival, 58, 64

Mellon, Thomas, 85

Méndez de Canzo, Gonzalo, 16, 27

Menéndez de Avilés, Pedro, 54, 72, 73, 83, 87, 88

Mexican War, 28

Mickler-O'Connell Bridge, 84

Mills, Robert, 27

Minorca, 21, 22, 94

Minorcan, 22, 47, 67, 94, 96

Mission of Nombre de Dios, 70, 72, **72**

Monumento de la Constitución (*see* Constitution Monument)

Moccasin Branch, 94

Model Land Company, 63, 64, 65

Model Land Company Historic District, 53, 64, **64**, 65

Moore, Carolina Governor James, 18

Moorish Revival Style, 54, 56, 58, 71

Moreno, Mariano, 42

Mosquitos, 105

Moultrie, 104

Moultrie, John,

Moultrie, Dr. John, Jr., 26, 104

Moultrie Creek, 93, 104, 106

Murat, Prince Charles Louis Napoleon Achille, 46

Museum of Florida's Military, 39

museums, 17, 23, 24, 27, 37, 38, 39, 40, 43, 46, 47, 54, 55, **55**, 58, 71, **71**, 74, 80

National Cemetery, 41, **41**

National Historic Landmark, 38

National Register of Historic Places, 33, 49, 59, 70, 74, 79

National Society of the Colonial Dames of the State of Florida, 37

National Trust for Historic Preservation, 45

Nativity of Our Lady of Tolomato, 98

New Smyrna Colony, 21, 22, 47, 94

New Smyrna Beach, 94, 105

New Switzerland, 107

New World, 29, 39, 99

O'Brien, Henry Stanton, 92

O'Brien-Kelley House, 92, **92**

Oglethorpe, General James, 78, 78, 97, 100, 107

Oglethorpe Battery Park, 78, **78**

Old Jail, 74, **75**

Old Kings Road, 105

"Old Spanish Inn," 23

Old Spanish Quarries, 82, **82**

Old Spanish Well and Chimney, 81, **81**

Old St. Augustine Village, 46, 47

Old World, 9

"Oldest House," (*see* González-Alvarez House)

"Oldest Schoolhouse," (*see* Genopoly House)

Operation Pastorius, 106

Order of Masons, 29

O'Reilly, Father Michael, 43

O'Reilly House, 43, **43**

Osceola, 104

Osceola Capture Site, 9, 104

Palace Market, 86

Palaica, 49

Palm Row, 34–35, 48, **48**

Pamies-Arango Cigar Company, 61

parapet, 18, 19, 30, 31

Paredes-Dodge House, 24, 25, **25**

Pascua Florida, 73

Patriot Rebellion of 1812, 107

Patroness of Motherhood, 72

Peavett, Mary Evans, 38

Peck, Dr. Seth, 26

Pellicer, Francisco, 96

Peña, Juan Esteban de, 26

Peña-Peck House, 26, **26**

Philip II, King, 88

Picolata, 41, 99, 100, **100**, **101**, 106

pirate(s), 72

P.J. Pauley Jail Building and Manufacturing Company, 74

Plant, Henry B., 63

plantation(s), 49, 84, 96, 97, 104, 105, 107

Plaza de la Constitución (*see* Colonial Town Plaza)

Pocotalaca, 49

Ponce de Leon Hotel (Flagler College), **2**, 9, 54, 57, **57**, 58, 60, 63, 64, 65, 66, 74, 92

Ponte Vedra, 106,

Pope John Paul II, 51

Potato Growers Building, 95

poured concrete, 54, 56, 58, 66, 92

Presbyterian, 20, 62, 63

Prince Murat House, 46, **46**, 47

Price, Eugenia, 37, 38

Protestant, 20, 29, 32, 51, 88

Public Burying Ground (Huguenot Cemetery), 20, **20**

Queen Anne style, 44, 59, 92

queen of Spain, 27

quoins, 95

Rawlings, Marjorie Kinnan, 71

redoubt, 18

Renwick, James, 30

reptiles, 79

Restoration Area, 16, 17, **17**, 19, 21, 24, 25

Revolutionary War (*see* American Revolution)

Richardson, Henry Hobson, 65

Ripley, Robert, 71

Ripley's "Believe It or Not!" Museum (*see* Warden Castle)

Rockefeller, John D., 54, 71

Rodríguez-Avero-Sánchez House, 24, **24**, 25

Roman Catholic, 29, 30, 43, 51

Romanelli, F., 33

Romanesque Revival style, 65, 74

Roosevelt, President Franklin D., 106

Rosario Line, 18, 19

Royal Governor, 27, 28

Royal Highway (see Camino Real)

Salt Run, 83
Sánchez, don Juan, 23
Sanford, General Henry, 63
Santo Domingo Redoubt, 18
Schladermundt, Herman T., 62
Scott, General Winfield, 100
Second Seminole War, 11, 18, 19, 41, 93, 96, 100, 104, 106
Second Spanish Period, 11, 21, 29, 30, 36, 43, 46, 98, 107
Seguí–Kirby Smith House, 36, **36**, 37
Seloy, 72
Seminoles, 11, 93, 104, 106
sentry tower, 31, 80
Sherman, William Tecumseh, 100
Sisters of the Blessed Sacrament, 51
Sisters of St. Joseph, 43, 45, 94
Smith, Franklin W., 56, 58
Smith, Peter Sken, 70
Solla, Augustine, 61
Solla-Carcaba Cigar Factory, 53, 61, **61**
Spanish Colonial
    periods, 24, 51
    architecture, 14, 25, 36
Spanish Parliament, 29
Spanish Renaissance Revival style, 66
Spanish Royal Treasury, 23
St. Ambrose Catholic Church, 94, **94**
St. Ambrose Parish, 94
St. Augustine Alligator Farm, 79, **79**, 82, 83
St. Augustine Beach, 79, 83
St. Augustine Historical Society, 25, 36, 38, 39, 42
St. Augustine Historical Society and Institute of Science (see St. Augustine Historical Society)
St. Augustine Improvement Company, 71
St. Augustine Lighthouse and Keeper's Quarters, 80, **80**
St. Augustine Quadricentennial, 72
St. Benedict the Moor Church, 51, **51**

St. Cyprian's Episcopal Church, 7, 50, **50**
St. Francis Barracks, 40, **40**, 41
St. Johns County, 9, 10, 36, 39, 81, 82, 85, 86, 92, 94, 95, 96, 99, 100, 104, 105, 106, 107
St. Johns County Board of County Commissioners, 56, 74
St. Johns River, 20, 41, 88, 100, 101, 104, 107
St. Joseph's Academy, 67
St. Patrick's Cathedral, 30
St. Photios Shrine (see Avero House)
state of Florida, 17, 27, 37, 40, 83, 86, 96, 97, 98
steel, 72, 85
stucco, 23, 46
Summer Haven, 85, **85**
Surprise Store, 59
Switzerland, 99, 107

tabby, 43
Tallahassee, 19, 46
terra cotta, 31, 54, 62, 66
Territorial Period, 37, 47
Theatrical Troupe Massacre Site, 9, 106
Tiffany, Louis Comfort, 32, 57
Tocoi, 99
Tolomato Cemetery, 42, 53, 67, **67**
tourism, 15, 20, 79, 105
tourist(s), 37, 83, 85
    attraction, 23, 74
    destination, 79
    industry, 25, 95
    and transportation, 64, 74, 105
Tovar, José, 39
Tovar House, 39, **39**
Town Plan, 28
Treaty of Moultrie Creek, 93, 104, 106
Treaty Park, 93, **93**
Trinity Episcopal Church, 7, 32, **32**
Turnbull, Dr. Andrew, 47

Union Army, 39, 100

University of Florida, 48, 79
Upham, Colonel John, 44
U.S. Army, 41, 104
U.S. Army Corps of Engineers, 83
U.S. Coast Guard, 80
U.S. Congress, 36, 96
U.S. Department of the Interior, 14, 49
U.S. National Park Service, 14, 18, 87
U.S. Senate, 93
U.S. War Department, 14, 40

Varela, Father Felix, 67
Verot, Bishop Jean Pierre Augustin Marcellin, 67
Victorian Era, 40, 55
    architecture, 48, 64, 70
    buildings, 49
Villa Zorayda (Zorayda Castle), 53, 56, 58, **58**, 71, 92
Visitor Information Center, 14, 15, **15**, 16, 17, 19, 20, 27, 67, 71

Walton Company, 84
Warden, William G., 71
Warden Castle (Ripley's "Believe It or Not!" Museum), 71, **71**
Washington Monument, 27
West Florida, 11
West Point, 36
Whipple, Reverend Benjamin, 32
White, Mrs. Loomis L., 50
William Bartram Trail, 99, **99**
Woman's Exchange Club, 26
Works Progress Administration (WPA), 15, 27
Wright's Landing, 98

Xavier Lopez House, 53, 59, **59**
Ximenez, Andres, 37
Ximenez-Fatio House, 37, **37**

Zorayda Castle (see Villa Zorayda)

Here are some other books from Pineapple Press on related topics. For a complete catalog, write to Pineapple Press, P.O. Box 3889, Sarasota, Florida 34230-3889, or call (800) 746-3275. Or visit our website at www.pineapplepress.com.

St. Augustine

Houses of St. Augustine by David Nolan. Photographs by Ken Barrett Jr., watercolors by Jean Ellen Fitzpatrick. The complete and fully illustrated book of the architecture of the Spanish, British, and American periods. Full color. (hb & pb)

Flagler's St. Augustine Hotels by Thomas Graham. Describes Henry Flagler's three lavish hotels in St. Augustine: the Ponce de Leon, Flagler's preeminent hotel, now houses Flagler college; the Alcazar now holds the City Hall and Lightner Museum; the Casa Monica (previously called the Cordova) has been restored as a hotel. Full-color photographs. (pb)

Menéndez: Pedro Menéndez de Avilés, Captain General of the Ocean Sea by Albert Manucy. A complete and accurate biography of Pedro Menéndez de Avilés, the founder of the nation's oldest city, St. Augustine. Based on scholarly research, this book portrays the life of a leader whose ambition drove him to pursue adventure and conquest. (hb)

St. Augustine Ghosts

Ghosts of St. Augustine by Dave Lapham. Illustrated by Tom Lapham. The unique and often turbulent history of America's oldest city is told in twenty-four spooky stories that cover four hundred years' worth of ghosts. (pb)

Ancient City Hauntings by Dave Lapham. Illustrated by Tom Lapham. In this sequel to *Ghosts of St. Augustine,* the author takes you on more quests for supernatural experiences through the dark, enduring streets of the Ancient City. Come visit the Oldest House, the Old Jail, Ripley's, the Oldest School House, and all the many haunted B&Bs and other establishments that harbor wandering souls and spirits from ancient times. (pb)

Oldest Ghosts by Karen Harvey. In St. Augustine the ghost apparitions are as intriguing as the city's history. Meet a Colonial-period ghost who hangs laundry in a Spanish courtyard, the ghosts of Will Green and Judge John Stickney, and many other. (pb)

Florida

Historic Homes of Florida, 2nd edition, by Laura Stewart and Susanne Hupp. Houses tell the human side of history. In this survey of restored residences, their stories are intertwined with those of their owners in a domestic history of Florida. Most of these houses are museums now; others are restaurants or bed-and-breakfasts. This new edition is updated and illustrated with color photographs. (pb)

Historical Traveler's Guide to Florida, 2nd edition, by Eliot Kleinberg. From Fort Pickens in the Panhandle to Fort Jefferson in the ocean 40 miles beyond Key West, historical travelers will find many adventures waiting for them in Florida. The author presents 74 of his favorites—17 of them are new to this edition, and the rest have been completely updated. (pb)